London Is Forced To Show Its Hand

CLEARING THE FOG OF WAR

Lies, Damn Lies, Damn British Lies

The Lyndon LaRouche Political Action Committee issued this appeal on Apr. 16. EIR *wants to associate itself with this call, and advises our readers to take it as a guide for their thinking in these critical days.*

The *Washington Post* this morning portrays President Trump as surrounded by a traitorous foreign policy team which is lying to him constantly and persistently about Russia, and about actions this team has taken in the President's name, in your name, against Russia and China. The *Post* attempts to claim that Trump's national security staff staged a palace coup against him concerning Russia and Syria, and that Trump has lost the battle.

But the President responded immediately by acting against the traitors around him. He scuttled the appointment of Nikki Haley's assistant, the Never-Trumper Jon Lemer, for a national security post with Mike Pence. The White House announced that new sanctions against Russia based on Russia's support for Syria, which Nikki Haley promoted only yesterday, were being rolled back. It was publicly announced that President Trump still wants to meet with Vladimir Putin, although a date has not yet been set.

At the same time, French President Emmanuel Macron bragged to the world that it was he who duped the President into a missile attack on Syria, reviving the very Clinton/Obama '"regime-change" doctrines the American people righteously rejected in the 2016 elections. This only sets the stage for ferocious blowback on the President of France.

As the fog of last week's actions lifts, several aspects of our present situation are much, much clearer. While the Anglo-Americans fall all over themselves to stupidly declare they have caged Trump, it is very clear that their claimed victory is pyrrhic, arrogantly delusional, and temporary. They were reckless, and the blowback potential is enormous and revolutionary for the world, if the American people now join Lyndon LaRouche's call to cancel the British Empire. At no time since Franklin Roosevelt declared his intention to end British colonialism, has the Anglo-Dutch Empire been so fragile and exposed. Here are the relevant features of our present situation:

1. The Syria chemical attack hoax, the Skripal poisoning hoax in Britain, and the British-inspired coup against our President are all one British strategic package. Britain, with its long-time poodle France in tow, is now out to lead the Western world in challenging Russia and China, who are claimed to be practicing something called totalitarian capitalism. Here is how British imperial scribe Allister Heath described the British motive for the poisoning hoaxes in Salisbury and Syria in the March 14 London *Telegraph*:

We need a new world order to take on totalitarian capitalists in Russia and China…. Such an alliance would dramatically shift the global balance of power, and allow the liberal democracies finally to fight back. It would endow the world with the sorts of robust institutions that are required to contain Russia and China. Britain needs a new role in the world; building such a network would be our perfect mission.

Across the pond, as they say, at the very same time, a similar foundational statement was made by 68 former Obama Administration officials who have formed a group called National Security Action, aimed at securing Donald Trump's impeachment and attacking Russia and China.

2. The Russians now say they have incontrovertible proof that the White Helmets, an aid organization associated with Al-Qaeda and funded to the tune of millions by the British government and USAID, staged the chemical attack in Douma, Syria, at the direct urging of London. The proof includes photographs and intercepts. At the same time, an independent Swiss laboratory working with the Organisation for the Prohibition of Chemical Weapons (OPCW) has stated that the poison used on the Skripals was something called BZ, an agent never developed in Russia but residing, instead, in the chemical weapons programs of both the United States and the UK. These claims are fully consistent with independent analysis LaRouche PAC has provided over the past 10 days. (See "There Was No Chemical Attack in Syria" and "Assad's Chemical Weapons: Another British Fairytale.")

3. Already in Great Britain, coming from the Labour Party and the Brexit movement, there is an enormous popular reaction against these lies. They appropriately compare the classified evidence for the poisoning hoaxes to the lies that led to the disastrous Iraq War. Similarly, here, the forgotten Americans who elected Trump to end this nonsense, joined with LaRouche PAC and protested loudly all last week against the Syria attack. That protest, by all accounts, pulled the world back from the nuclear brinksmanship and posturing fomented by Britain, France, and their Democratic Party and neocon colleagues in the United States.

4. A major driving force in this situation is the impending financial collapse of the Wall Street and City of London financial centers. Far from practicing totalitarian capitalism, China, joined with Russia, is on a massive infrastructure-building and economic development project joined by over 100 other nations in the world. It is the largest infrastructure-building project ever undertaken by human beings, and it has the express aim of ending poverty and raising living standards throughout the planet. China and Russia are also dedicating significant portions of their budgets to space exploration and fundamental scientific discovery. This is the kind of big thinking we in the United States used to engage in. It echoes the American system of political economy. Totalitarian capitalism, it is not.

If President Trump accepts China's invitation to join the United States to the Belt and Road Initiative, then the Anglo-Dutch Empire, rather than Donald Trump, will be consigned to the dustbin of history.

5. The situation remains fraught with danger. Nikki Haley and John Bolton have committed the United States to a military response any time a terrorist in Syria can stage another phony chemical attack. Ukraine is another possible trigger point by those engaged in treason against our country and our President. It is also now clear that a desperate Robert Mueller is out to turn Donald Trump's lawyer into state's evidence against his client, a tactic the filthy Mueller has repeatedly used. Mueller's tactic, this time, just may have eliminated the Sixth Amendment to the U.S. Constitution. Mueller is desperate, because Russiagate has blown up, Comey is a flop, and whole sections of the Obama Justice Department are now racing to expose one another's crimes.

So, as the fog clears, we find ourselves actually on the edge of victory. The question will be decided by the courage of the people of the United States to demand and to act to end the coup, to expose the perfidious British lies, and insisting on getting on with rebuilding the country and the planet. Lyndon LaRouche warned constantly against pragmatism in just such a situation. Citing the words of St. Paul, LaRouche reminds us, "For we wrestle not against flesh and blood, but against principalities, against powers, against the rulers of the darkness of this world, against spiritual wickedness in high places." (Ephesians 6:12) Be a force for the righteous and the good.

Join us in this battle. Tell the President to investigate and fully expose the perfidious French and British lies. Call the White House (202) 456-1111. Tell the Congress: End the coup or your career will end at the ballot box in 2018! (202) 224-3121

EIR Contents

www.larouchepub.com   Volume 45, Number 16, April 20, 2018

Cover This Week

LONDON IS FORCED TO SHOW ITS HAND

INCONVENIENT PROOF

London Finance Dominates the World, Ruins Economies, Including America's

by Paul Gallagher

The Spider's Web: Britain's Second Empire
Documentary film, 2017
Produced by Michael Oswald and John
Christensen; 69 minutes.

April 15—After two years of a British dossier driving an attempted coup against President Donald Trump, and as the British government of Theresa Mayhem is attempting to force the President into a potentially unsurvivable confrontation with Russia, the recently released documentary, *The Spider's Web*, demonstrates the full destructive power of the British Empire—today.

This unusual film will prove those wrong who believe Britain long since ceased to be an empire and has become just a clever manipulator, or even a "puppy" of the great power of the United States. And likewise, those who think Britain's offshore banking havens such as the Cayman Islands represent a manageable problem like Swiss banking secrecy, and are an obsession only of economic equality/tax justice crusaders.

What is proven here is rather the truth insisted on by Lyndon LaRouche and *EIR* for many years. Not only is London the central driver of geopolitical manipulations, coups, and wars against rival or rising powers. London is also the world's dominant financial power and has held the whip hand in making speculation, securitization, and drug-and-terror financing the main activities of global banking since the late 1960s.

Drawing the World's Wealth to London

The Spider's Web is co-produced by Tax Justice Network founder John Christensen, and is based in part on a 2011 book, *Treasure Islands*, by expert on British offshore havens Nicholas Shaxson; an interview with Shaxson is one of its major elements. Christensen has the expertise of having "gone under cover" as advisor to the Queen's government of the island of Jersey for a number of years.

The film is being screened in a "film tour" by Christensen in the UK and Germany in April-May-June, but has no viewings scheduled in the United States.

It lays bare the tremendous damage the City of London and its banks have done to the world economy—and the U.S. economy—since the 1960s. In its title, its creators are not referring to a *secondary* British empire, but to the re-establishment of *the* British Empire after its decisive military demise in the 1950s.

The workings of the UK's dependent territories, the

island financial havens Jersey, Guernsey, British Virgin Islands, Cayman Islands, Gibraltar, formerly Bahamas, etc. have been notorious for years. But the documentary's broad overview successfully creates an entirely different understanding of them for the viewer. London's havens, run directly by the Bank of England and City of London, have been drawing the assets of the world *into the City of London's banks* for 50 years. This has made London again globally dominant financially, able to loot the developing countries and to drive the U.S. economy, among others, toward speculation over lending, "financialization," highly risky "securitization," and deregulation of Wall Street.

The film's experts show that London has been able to drive *deindustrialization* of the American and European economies, particularly since London's "Big Bang" financial deregulation of October 1986, which called the shots for trans-Atlantic bank deregulation.

Moreover, by establishing the "bolt holes"—the Bank of England's own word for tax-evading island wealth-sinks—and the rules enabling financial corporations and multinationals to pay minimal taxes, and wealthy individuals none at all, London has driven wealth inequality to unprecedented levels, gorgeously rewarded non-productive investment of nations' savings, and triggered the growth of populism in opposition.

In short, London has driven down growth, productivity, and productive lending and investment in economies throughout the world for half a century. This is the same half-century in which productivity growth and technological breakthroughs have slowed to a virtual stop in the United States economy—to the great puzzlement of economists; its active workforce has begun to shrink; and wars and drug addictions have taken over.

It is now—though neither Shaxson's book nor the film take up *this* subject—being partially reversed by China's extraordinary growth and outward productive investment during this century. London and Beijing represent opposite paradigms for the world economy.

The Places Called 'Elsewhere'

The Spider's Web presents a straightforward narrative of the creation of the "Second British Empire."

Begin with Clement Atlee, British Prime Minister 1945-51: "Over and over we have seen that there is another power than that which has its seat at Westminster.

The City of London, a convenient term for a collection of financial interests, is able to assert itself vs. the government of the country."

The original haven was London itself, from the 1960s. Against the stability of Franklin Roosevelt's post-War Bretton Woods system, London invented "offshore," and the City of London was "offshore"—the place where Bretton Woods regulations were not followed, and where the Bretton Woods regulations were finally destroyed by the illegally high interest rates of the "Eurodollar" market by the early 1970s.

The Bank of England (BoE) in 1966 declared dollar operations *in London* out of its jurisdiction; they were officially occurring "Elsewhere." "London," says Shaxson, "was a place where senior bankers did not have to worry about the consequences of their actions" (as Wall Street has become since the 1990s). Wall Street banks all moved their international operations to London, where they remain. The "euromarket," centered in London, rose to $500 billion in size by 1980; to $4.8 trillion by 1988; and 90% of international loans worldwide were made through this market by 1997.

Starting by licensing the Bank of Credit and Commerce International, or BCCI, in 1972, the Bank of England harbored and protected banks funding terrorism and drugs—BCCI became the world's 7th-largest bank within a decade of its founding, then went bankrupt. The BoE knew BCCI was financing drug cartels and terrorist groups, but tried to prevent its failure. When it failed and its crimes spilled out, then BOE Governor Robert Leigh-Pemberton said, "If we closed down a bank every time we found an incidence of fraud, we'd have rather fewer banks here than we do at the moment."

The BoE recommended governors for what it called the "secrecy jurisdictions" (offshore islands and island groups) to the British government, which appointed them. London has complete control of these havens while claiming in every instance that it has none; again,

John Christensen, co-producer of The Spider's Web: Britain's Second Empire.

they are "Elsewhere." When the Bahamas, for example, *actually* left British control and became independent, financial firms all left there and went to the Cayman Islands.

The London banks all set up operations in the offshore havens. London law firms and accounting firms threw many thousands of their most skilled personnel into designing ever-more-complicated "offshore secrecy structures." These networks, of trusts owning corporations owning trusts, etc., allow ownership of assets to be completely concealed, while allowing them to earn high rates of return, *and allowing this growing wealth back into the global financial system — through London banks.* A Jersey Senator/whistleblower, who has been repeatedly imprisoned, states that in the City of London and offshore havens, "Most politicians are in business" — the business of designing and executing trust structures.

The purpose was to funnel the world's wealth to the City of London. Beginning with Chase Manhattan about 1970, London has cut U.S.-based major banks in on the wealth flows, thereby contributing to American deindustrialization and bank deregulation (above all, the repeal of the Glass-Steagall Act).

But at present, 25% of the world's financial activity, and 50% of financial derivatives betting, is conducted on British territory (the United States has 19% and 25%). Three-quarters of the world's hedge funds are registered in the Caymans alone.

A stunning example of the accomplishment of the Second Empire is presented by Christensen in a chalkboard presentation: "As much as $50 trillion in assets in the world are owned by no one." Whether casinos, investment funds or racehorses, their beneficial ownership is virtually impossible to establish. Thus they pay taxes only voluntarily if at all.

The Bank of England apparently *could* publish a registry of trusts and their owners, but does not allow it. (The film's account of the doings of HMRC—Her Majesty's Revenue Commission, the British "IRS"—has to be watched to be believed.)

The Cause Behind the Screen

Nothing is more valuable about this new film than its revelation of Britain's Second Empire as the cause—unseen but by an exceptional few—of great economic changes for the worse in the past half-century.

Capital flight from developing countries is $1 trillion per year, and *half* goes into the London-centered banking system. Over the period 1970-2008, $944 billion in capital flight from sub-Saharan Africa alone went into UK offshore secrecy jurisdictions. Developing countries looted in this way, by the terribly powerful incentive for their elites which "offshore" represents, are robbed of investment, development, and *de facto* are huge creditors of City of London banks.

Productive investment in the industrialized countries of Europe and North America has been disincentivized at all levels, because it is regulated and taxed, while non-productive and securitized investment, particularly FIRE investment ("Financial Independence and Retiring Early"), has the offshore world at its disposal, unregulated and untaxed. These nations' governments, too, are no match for London's "Elsewhere" when it comes to the revenue with which they invest in technological progress and infrastructure.

The offshore havens are drivers of economic inequality in nations all over the world.

Many attacks are launched against "Russian mafia" and "Russian oligarchs" as evil financial forces; but since as long ago as the late 1950s, Russians with wealth have been but fish in the sea of London "offshore" finance, often drawn to live in London and sometimes entrapped there. British Prime Minister David Cameron's father, for example, designed secret trusts for such as these Russians to invest in.

London as the cause behind the screen—for the replacement of bank separation by bank deregulation, the looting of the developing countries, disinvestment in production, creation of "the 1%," terror financing—is exposed in *The Spider's Web*. Britain's Second Empire is what the new paradigm of the New Silk Road has emerged to replace. Reinstatement of Glass-Steagall alone would begin the Empire's destruction.

British False-Flag Provocations Put War Danger at 'Red Alert' Level

This is the edited transcript of the April 12, 2018 Schiller Institute New Paradigm webcast, an interview with the founder of the Schiller Institutes, Helga Zepp-LaRouche. She was interviewed by Harley Schlanger. A video *of the webcast is available.*

Harley Schlanger: Hello. I'm Harley Schlanger with the Schiller Institute. Welcome to today's international webcast featuring our founder Helga Zepp-LaRouche.

Since Monday, our organization has been on a Red Alert status, given the escalation of the danger of all-out war breaking out, following the most recent provocations coming from the British empire. Helga, earlier this week, issued a statement saying that we are sitting on a powder keg—with threats to go to war against Syria; to attack or even punish Assad; even possibly to punish the Russians, as President Trump indicated in a tweet earlier this week. We're still sitting on that powder keg. Despite being ill, Helga is here for a brief period, to present a strategic overview and the strategy for the mobilization to stop the escalating war danger. So, Helga, I turn it over to you now.

Helga Zepp-LaRouche: We are indeed in a very dangerous situation, which could get out of control very rapidly. To underline the point: President Trump's tweet directed at Russia, which made the headlines internationally, that "missiles will be coming." That turns out to be a reaction to fake news! The background of this story is, that about a week ago, Alexander Zasypkin, the Russian ambassador to Lebanon, gave an interview saying that any attack on Syria would be answered by a full military reaction by Russia.

It turns out that that interview, which appeared on Hezbollah TV (Al Manar) and was translated into

▲ A video released by the Syrian civil defence force White Helmets shows medical workers treating children after the attack on Douma Photograph: AP

Patrick Wintour *and* **Ewen MacAskill** *in London,* **Julian Borger** *in Washington and* **Angelique Chrisafis** *in Paris*

Arabic, was mistranslated. Zasypkin had, in fact, referred to an earlier remark by General Valery Gerasimov, the Chief of Staff of the Armed Forces of Russia, who in March warned that Moscow would shoot down missiles fired towards Syria and would target their launch sites, if the attacks threatened members of the Russian army. So, it was not that *any* attack on Syria would be met with a Russian retaliation, but only if the lives of Russian soldiers were threatened, which is a huge difference.

That false story was the trigger for Trump's tweet, starkly pointing out that in this environment of complete orchestration of fake news, false flag attacks, and secret service manipulations of all kinds, how easy it is to stage an incident and how things can get out of control.

We are not out of the danger of war. It's still unclear what will happen. At yesterday's White House press briefing, Press Secretary Sarah Sanders said about Syria, "We're maintaining that we have a number of options, and all of these options are still on the table." According to media reports, which are not very reliable, but it's the only source we have—British Prime Minister Theresa met with her cabinet, supposedly to decide if the British would participate in a U.S. military attack. The U.S. warship *USS Donald Cook* is loitering somewhere around 100 km off Tartus, the Russian military port in Syria, and, the *USS Harry Truman* carrier group of seven warships left Naval Station Norfolk yesterday, presumably on its way to the Eastern Mediterranean.

Since Russia has full control of the air space over Syria, and the Syrian government has also extremely effective missile defense systems, should the United States launch a missile strike on Syria, it could very well lead to a confrontation between the two nuclear powers—the United States and Russia. So I can only urge all of you who are watching this program: Join our mobilization. Wherever you may be in the world, get your congressmen or your deputies to speak out in their legislative bodies to make sure that governments everywhere completely distance themselves from this madness. Demand a public debate and investigation. We must really have a total mobilization against this war danger.

Continuous Toilet Tissue of Lies

Schlanger: It's really important that people have a sense of the continuity of this threat. It started with the fake news from Theresa May and Boris Johnson, accusing the Russians of trying to poison Sergei Skripal, the former spy, and his daughter. That fell apart when the British chemical warfare experts at Porton Down declared they could not determine the origin of the chemical weapon used against the Skripals; thus they could not affirmatively say that it was from Russia. As soon as that fake news fell apart, the escalation began, with the claims of so-called chemical weapons having been in East Ghouta, in Douma, Syria.

That occurred at precisely the point that Donald Trump said he's prepared to pull the United States troops out of Syria entirely. I think it is important, Helga, for you to go through what some Russians, including Russian President Putin, have been saying on this. There have been Russian statements saying that it's very obvious that this is a scripted assault against

Russia steps up rhetoric over Douma 'chemical attack'

Suspected chemical attack near Damascus dismissed as 'staged' by West during emergency session at UN Security Council.

Russia has described the actions of the US concerning Syria as 'reckless' [Eduardo Munoz/Reuters]

The UN Security Council has held an emergency meeting called by Russia to discuss what it describes as a threat to international peace from potential US

MORE ON SYRIA'S CIVIL WAR

What media in Russia, Iran

Russia and against Trump.

So what are we hearing from the Russians?

Zepp-LaRouche: The First Deputy Chief of the General Staff of Russia has just reported that Russian Atomic-Biological-Chemical (ABC) warfare specialists have been, or are in Douma, inspecting both the material of the so-called chemical weapons and also the patients in the hospital. They confirmed what representatives of the Red Crescent Society had said earlier, that there was absolutely no trace of chemical weapons, and also no sign that any patients in the hospital had been injured by such a weapon.

That again points to the fact that all the information about this so-called incident came from a group called the White Helmets, an organization funded by the British government and also, in part, by the U.S. State Department's Agency for International Development (USAID). Several whistleblowers have documented that the White Helmets are very close to the jihadists, and that that group completely staged this chemical weapons incident.

Russian Foreign Minister Sergey Lavrov said that Russia had, for the last month, seen signs of a planned provocation and that Russian authorities had provided

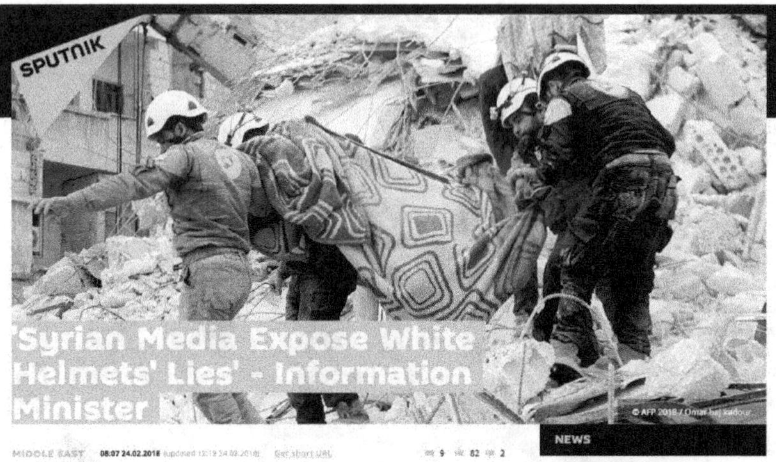

The ongoing hideous information war against Syria is not going to end with the victory over terrorists on the battlefield, the country's Information Minister Imad Sarah told Sputnik.

that information to both the UN Security Council and the Organization for the Prohibition of Chemical Weapons (OPCW). It was thus known *in advance* that an attack of this sort was in preparation, and also that the jihadists had dug tunnels under various cities, from which they were operating with explosive materials, mixed with chemical weapons. This is such an obvious case of a false-flag operation, that if it is used for a pretext to launch an attack, then we're really already in World War III, because this is designed to target Russia. I would even say that it did not start with the Skripal case; it started with the Russiagate coup attempt against President Trump, which has completely fallen apart.

The Skripal case also has fallen apart. The OPCW was just in Salisbury, England, investigating the material used in the attack on the Skripals. The OPCW team concluded its investigation, saying that it was not able to go beyond the UK laboratory report; they could not identify the origin of the nerve agent.

The OPCW—in its whole purpose of existence— has visited every laboratory in every country and has samples of every chemical substance, every nerve agent, so its experts can compare the agent used in the Skripal case with their own samples. The substance could not be identified as originating from Russia. So it didn't come from Russia. This case is also falling apart.

I do think it's really important that people see the continuity, as you say, Harley, of these lies, which are designed as preparation for a war against Russia. There is

no other explanation possible.

Bring the War Criminals to Justice

Schlanger: It's a war against Russia that's designed to sabotage President Trump's policy of working with Russian President Putin to cooperate against terrorism and, as Trump noted in one of his tweets, for economic cooperation with Russia.

U.S. Defense Secretary, General James Mattis, is also urging caution, saying we have to wait until we can see that there's some evidence of this attack in Syria. Mattis came out after the March 2017 false flag incident, which led to a U.S. attack, saying there was no evidence of chemical weapons, or that it was the Assad government. So we're seeing a certain amount of back-peddling. Very importantly, the former British Ambassador to Syria, Peter Ford, and also the former UK Ambassador to Uzbekistan, Craig Murray, both of whom have been very outspoken on this latest alleged incident, warned that this is a crazy escalation to war.

What should people do? Many people are now speaking out and asking what can be done. What are we doing as part of our mobilization?

Zepp-LaRouche: We have various appeals—one in Germany which you will find in German on our web-

DoD/U.S. Army Sgt. Amber I. Smith
From left, James Mattis, Secretary of Defense, and Gen. Joseph Dunford, Jr., Chairman of the Joint Chiefs of Staff, briefing reporters at the Pentagon on the evening of the April 13 U.S., UK, and French air strikes on Syria.

German Chancellor Angela Merkel and French President François Macron.

site there, and we have one on the American site of our colleagues at LaRouche PAC. These appeals should be used to mobilize every parliament around the world. In the United States, our colleagues there are in a red-alert mobilization. They have already distributed tens of thousands of leaflets; they have contacted everyone in the U.S. Congress in Washington, D.C. directly. We're doing similar things in Europe. We really have to take the war danger very seriously.

Germany's former highest ranking military officer, Gen. Harald Kujat, gave interviews today to three different TV stations, making the point, which I can only fully endorse, that we are confronted with a political class incapable of calculating the consequences of their deeds, and that therefore the danger is that they will sleepwalk into a third World War, just as happened in the case of the First World War.

I may not share all the reasons why he thinks this is happening now. He attributes this situation to an unfortunate combination of an inexperienced French President, a Prime Minister in Great Britain who has tremendous domestic problems, and an erratic American President.

He, however, blasts the German government, saying that rather than trying to calm the situation down, German Chancellor Merkel is actually heating it up! This is incredible! Germany was virtually destroyed *twice* in world wars. How could our Chancellor immediately defend UK Prime Minister May in her unsubstantiated accusations and immediately assert that Assad is guilty? General Kujat put Merkel on the spot and demanded that she intervene against the rush to war.

I think that the problem is that these politicians are really incapable of seeing the implications of what they are doing. We need a full-fledged, in-depth mobilization of all parliamentarians in every country. Our listeners should use our materials and demand that their governments, and all governments, denounce these false-flag operations and oppose this rush to war.

Let me highlight the fact that the German judge, Peter Vonnahme, a Bavarian court judge until 2007, pointed to the continuity in all of these provocations, the obvious aim being regime change in Russia. He then asked these pointed questions: Have people forgotten the Gulf of Tonkin incident, which led to the Vietnam War, or the false allegations of babies being ripped out of incubators in Kuwait, which led to the pretext to attack Iraq in 1990, or the fake Niger "yellowcake" story claiming that Saddam Hussein bought yellowcake uranium to produce weapons of mass destruction, which was then used as a pretext for war against Iraq in 2003? Or, the so-called "Operation Horseshoe" incident, which led to the Kosovo intervention in 1999?

All these stories were fabricated and widely dissemi-

UK Prime Minister Theresa May.

Former British Prime Minister Tony Blair.

nated in a deliberately orchestrated fashion. We must have a public discussion: Who did that? Former British Prime Minister Tony Blair's "apology" for the Iraq war is not sufficient. These wars have cost *millions* of lives! It is high time that those responsible be called to justice. This injustice is too much and has been going on for too long!

Schlanger: I'm glad you mentioned Tony Blair, because he's one of the people saying that UK Prime Minister Theresa May doesn't have to go to the Parliament: She should immediately join the coalition with Macron and Trump, and start bombing Syria. Blair is a war criminal whose time has come to be brought before a tribunal.

The picture wouldn't be complete without going back to what you said was the initial phase, which is Russiagate. There was a development, right in the middle of the Syria mobilization, with the U.S. Attorney for the Southern District of New York launching an FBI raid on the offices and home of Donald Trump's personal attorney, Michael Cohen, for allegations referred to that U.S. Attorney by Special Counsel Robert Mueller, which have *nothing whatsoever* to do with Russiagate.

We've basically said that this is part of a blackmail operation against Trump. How do you see this functioning?

With Determination and Humor

Zepp-LaRouche: I think it discredits Mueller even more. It's very obvious that Russiagate is falling apart. Mueller has therefore shifted to new areas, way beyond his mandate as Special Counsel. His new move is a fishing expedition focused on a sex story, that Trump was supposedly involved with a porn movie star. This is so out of order, that I think it will fall back on Mueller.

The reaction of the famous Harvard lawyer, Alan Dershowitz, are also very important. He said that this is a violation of the U.S. Constitution, the Fourth and the Sixth Amendments. Dershowitz, a Democrat, is blasting the silence of the Democrats and especially the silence of the American Civil Liberties Union (ACLU). He said, "This is a black day for attorney-client relations," and that it is one of the many things that must be rectified.

Congressman Devin Nunes had to go as far as threatening to start impeachment proceedings against FBI Director Christopher Wray and Deputy Attorney General Rod Rosenstein, for blocking the release of documents subpoenaed by the House Judiciary and Oversight committees. Two critical pages, which had been demanded, were finally released in mostly unredacted form, with reference to the origins of the Trump investigation. We expect to hear more on that front.

Let me reiterate my appeal to all of our listeners: Mobilize with the Schiller Institute. Join the Schiller Institute, become an active member. It is very important that we build a movement to stop this war danger and create a New Paradigm of decent relations among all nations on this planet, particularly with Russia and China. That is absolutely possible, as we have discussed many times on this show.

More people need to become active to make this work. Therefore, I again invite you: Join the Schiller Institute and help us in this mobilization.

Schlanger: Make calls to the White House and to the U.S. Congress at 202-224-2131. There are congressmen, including Thomas Massie (R-Ky.) and others, who are demanding that nothing be done [regarding military action against Syria] without the Congress being consulted.

Let me also mention that in spite of the danger of the situation, it's good to see there are some people who have maintained their sense of humor: Maria Zakharova, the spokesperson for the Russian Foreign Ministry, in response to President Trump's tweet about "smart" missiles, said that if those missiles are really "smart" they'll go after the terrorists who are responsible for the false flag chemical weapons scare.

Helga, thanks for taking the time to join us today and making the effort, despite your illness, to present this strategic picture and mobilization. We are still on Red Alert. It is significant that you took the time to join us here. Is there anything more you want to add?

Zepp-LaRouche: No, I think that's what we have to do.

Schlanger: OK, very good. So we'll see you next week.

Zepp-LaRouche: OK, till next week.

There Was No Chemical Attack in Syria

William Wertz of LaRouche PAC interviewed Virginia State Senator Richard Black on April 11, 2018. The transcript follows.

Will Wertz: I am Will Wertz with the LaRouche Political Action Committee. We are here today to interview Virginia State Senator Richard Black, who is a retired Colonel in the U.S. Army. He also served as a Major in the U.S. Army Judge Advocate General's (JAG) Corps, and later headed the Army's Criminal Law Division in the Pentagon.

Virginia State Senator Richard Black, left, and William Wertz.

LPAC TV

He has had extraordinary experience in Syria, which he has visited a number of times. The purpose of this interview is to get Senator Black's views on the current crisis surrounding the allegation of a chemical weapons attack in East Ghouta, in the city of Douma, Syria.

Sen. Richard Black: I've been watching this very closely—I think all of us have. We are concerned because President Trump has surrounded himself by war cabinet. When he chose John Bolton as National Security Advisor—John Bolton is as extreme as anybody that you can find in the foreign policy arena—he chose someone who is very much an extremist when it comes to war. Bolton was one of the individuals who promoted the invasion of Iraq, which turned out to be based on false premises, and yet, here he is again. And he is an individual who is likely to call for war in many circumstances.

We have had this situation boiling up. It started several weeks ago, when the British began an hysterical media campaign, saying that the Syrian Army was going to use poison gas against the terrorists in the East Ghouta suburbs. This is a very large area, deep in the suburbs of Damascus, which is a sprawling city. The terrorists have held it since about 2012, and built a system of underground tunnels that they have used to keep control of the area. Whenever the Syrian government would try to restore order, the terrorists would emerge from their tunnels and ambush and slaughter anyone trying to restore order. So the terrorists have continued to hold it for all this time.

The British claimed that the Syrian Army, which had massed to finally eliminate the terrorist control of this Ghouta pocket, was going to use poisonous gas—and that it was going to happen imminently. As it turned out, the Syrian Army, led by the Tiger Forces, by the Republican Guard, and by other very elite groups, managed to burst through the enemy ranks by attacking from unexpected quarters, and rolled over the terrorists with such rapidity, that the Army was able to capture the major, terrorist-controlled chemical weapons facility. This apparently was the facility that was to be used to create incidents, in which the terrorists would fire on civilians, and then claim that it was the Syrian military forces attacking civilians. Once the terrorists lost this laboratory, they didn't have anything else to fight with.

Before long, a major part of the entire Ghouta pocket of terrorists simply evaporated. There was only one terrorist group left, Jaysh al-Islam, still holding the city of

Syrian Arab Army units in the southeastern countryside of Hama after defeating a group of Jabhat al-Nusra terrorists.

Douma. A little farther away there is another pocket, which is still totally held by ISIS. But all of the action right now is at Douma.

The Syrian Army attacked Douma and had similar success, breaking through all of the barriers that were there. Finally, Jaysh al-Islam agreed to conduct peace talks, and an agreement was reached that they would be permitted to relocate some of their people to other rebel-held areas. They asked that their severely wounded be evacuated by bus. The Syrian government sent in air-conditioned buses and evacuated the casualties first, followed by the fighters. They were not permitted to bring along their heavy weapons, but they could carry their side arms, automatic rifles, and so forth.

The evacuation was taking place: The battle for Ghouta was won. It was essentially over, and it was just a matter of arranging to evacuate the terrorist fighters. It has been the policy of Syria to cause as little damage to property and as little damage to human life as possible. And consequently, rather than duke it out to the bitter end, they simply allowed the terrorists to evacuate. They've done this throughout the war.

There have been a very small number of casualties; I think the United Nations estimate is about

British-financed, terrorist-allied White Helmets.

1,600 civilians have been killed, which, considering the magnitude of this battle, is very small.

Will the United States Defend ISIS?

We had a situation moving forward: The war was won, the terrorists were being evacuated, and then, the terrorists said, "Give us a truce so we can get some things arranged." Under the cover of that truce, the White Helmets, an arm of al-Qaeda, staged a provocative incident. Let me remind our viewers that al-Qaeda is the group that sent four civilian aircraft into the Twin Towers and the Pentagon, slaughtering 3,000 Americans on 9/11; that's what the White Helmets are part of. The White Helmets staged a provocative incident, portraying it as a poison gas attack. They claimed it was a sarin gas attack. Sarin gas is a colorless, odorless gas. If sarin gas were here in this room, today, we wouldn't know it, until we fell over. And yet, the claims are that people smelled chlorine.

Clearly, the terrorists don't entirely understand the chemistry of what they're working with. They mix up what chlorine gas is, which has a very strong characteristic aroma, and sarin gas.

But they made this claim, and immediately, just on cue, all of the major NATO powers said, "We've got to attack Syria." They never said, "We need to find out whether an attack occurred; and if it did, who caused it." It was just automatic—"OK, we've got to attack Syria."

It's clearly a pretext. I suspect it was a pretext that the British were involved in, because of their hysterics several weeks before the chemical laboratory was captured by the Syrian Army.

Now, here we are, on the verge of attacking Syria, *and it's not even clear that there was a chemi-*

A picture taken on April 8, 2018, shows Syrian Army soldiers gathering in an area on the eastern outskirts of Douma, as they continue their fierce offensive to retake the last opposition holdout

cal attack! There is a very credible—and we don't know for sure—but a very credible fellow, an English-speaking physician from the major hospital in Douma, who said, "We've never had any casualties brought in; we've never had any reports of poison gas, or anything of that sort." Now, if a chemical attack had occurred, certainly you would have had a flood of casualties— even if, let's say—their initial report was I think forty people had been killed. Even with that you'd have had a flood of people being brought into the hospital, and everybody would have known about it. Well, here's this physician reporting that he hadn't heard anything about such an event.

We don't even know that this happened! This may just simply be, much like Khan Sheikhoun, which was a propaganda ploy to get the United States to fire missiles, which we did—President Trump fired missiles. It's not clear, but we could be on the verge of attacking the good guys to help the bad guys. The final pocket of terrorists is being cleared out, and not by combat, but by emptying it out with buses, evacuating these people.

The residents, the people who live there, by the way, are ecstatic that they're finally released! They've been held hostage since 2012. And they're all reporting about how they were enslaved. Jaysh al-Islam was famous for building steel cages, putting women in them, and wherever they were staging an attack on Damascus by firing mortars or artillery, putting these cages filled with these women hostages, so that the Syrian Army couldn't respond in kind.

Now the terrorists are gone: The war for East Ghouta is over, and there remains only one small pocket still totally controlled by ISIS. And the United States is considering going in, and attacking the legitimate, duly elected, Syrian government, in order to prevent them from attacking this last pocket of ISIS in Damascus! *The idea that we would align ourselves with ISIS against the elected government, which clearly represents the people, is just astounding!*

British Lies and Manipulation

Wertz: Two questions: You mentioned the British role in this, and of course, the British were involved in the "dodgy dossier" that brought us to Iraq, under Tony Blair. We now have the Steele dossier which has been and is being used against the President of the United States, in the last year, which has unverified claims in it.

Black: False claims. I think most people, by this time, would say if you can't verify it after all this time, they're lies!

Wertz: Right. And then you have, the Skripal case, again involving the British, who refused to even allow a transparent investigation.

Black: And there is an international treaty that deals with how you deal with these things, and they refuse to abide by it. So it's basically, "It's our claim and you accept it. Don't look behind the screen." You know, "Ignore the man behind the screen."

Wertz: What do you think is occurring in terms of the British role in all of these situations? Of course, what's been pointed out, even by the Secretary General's Special Envoy to Syria, Staffan de Mistura, during the UN debate yesterday, are the international implications of a strike on Syria, when there are Russians present in Syria, who are vulnerable to such a strike. The Russians have warned that there will be consequences if there are Russian casualties, either accidentally or not. So, we're at a very, very dangerous situation, and the British are playing a very perfidious role in this whole situation. What's your sense of this?

Black: Let me tell you, Will, right now, the Western world—and the British are certainly instigators in this, but we certainly are not without blame; the French are certainly not— we have maneuvered ourselves to a point, where I think the degree of risk is as high as it was when the Archduke of Austria was assassinated, causing an explosion into the First World War—enormous bloodshed, suffering, destruction. And the First World War, of course, was sort of just a prelude to and laid the groundwork for the Second World War, and the vast destruction that took place.

We outspend Russia 11 to 1 on defense. Our defense budget is so big, that it equals the combined total of the next fourteen largest nations in terms of defense spending: Russia, China, Germany, Korea, and France; it just goes on and on. We have a *gargantuan* defense budget, and so we are more than a match for the Russians. The Russians, while they have a fine army, and fine military, it's much smaller. It just can't compare.

However, where we do have equality with Russia is with nuclear power. What makes the situation even worse today than the First World War, is that both the United States and Russia have roughly 1,500 nuclear weapons that are set to go, like that. And there are roughly 7,000 on either side, which are capable of being used in short order. That is enough probably to destroy two-thirds of humanity. And certainly the Western world, as we know it, would be practically annihilated: All of our major cities. Right here in Virginia, Naval Station Norfolk, the biggest naval base on Earth, would simply be gone. This Loudoun County which has huge Internet traffic would be gone. The Pentagon would be gone. New York City totally gone! It would totally be erased from the Earth!

We have people like Na-

cc/Michael Vadon

U.S. National Security Advisor John Bolton.

tional Security Advisor John Bolton, who are sufficiently reckless, to where, for their self-interest, they are willing to risk the death of perhaps 2 billion people, just simply purging them from the face of the Earth. It is incumbent on the President to recognize the extraordinary danger that we face.

We have been building up to this. Many of us elected Donald Trump on his promise that he was going to sort of normalize our relations with Russia; he was going to stop trying to overthrow President Assad, and work with the Syrians; he was going to downgrade the importance of NATO, and he was going to give up regime change. Trump has done a lot of the things he promised to do, *but he has not done one thing that he promised to do in foreign affairs.*

Well, you could take the exception—he was always very hostile towards the Iranian deal, and so he was honest about that. That's probably the one thing that he's focussed on most. Gen. Michael Flynn had been to be President Trump's National Security Advisor. Michael Flynn would have been a godsend for this nation. He knew where the skeletons are buried, he understood what was going on, and I think he recognized the importance of drawing back from nuclear war.

We have come to a point, probably more dangerous than any time in my lifetime—and I'm counting the time, when as kids we used to have air raid drills, and we'd get under our school desks, and our teachers would tell us to cover our eyes, so we wouldn't be blinded by the blast, and cover the back of our necks, so something wouldn't hit us and break our necks. People understood nuclear war then, because we had dropped the atomic bombs on Japan, and they understood what it could do. Today, it's sort of vague, it's very distant.

U.S. Air Force/Staff Sgt. Jonathan Lovelady

U.S. Army Lt. Gen. Michael Flynn, former director of the Defense Intelligence Agency.

But the nuclear weapons that we have today make the ones we used on Japan look like firecrackers. They're nothing! So we are at a fantastically perilous juncture in our history, and someone needs to take control of it, and say, "Let's pull back from the precipice."

Pushing Trump into War

Wertz: You raised the case of General Flynn, and President Trump's intentions for better relations with Russia, and his opposition to regime change. It seems very much, that he's been thwarted from carrying that out, by the British-instigated coup attempt against his administration, which has been going on for over a year, really, as he said yesterday, going all the way back to shortly after he was nominated.

Black: You're right. The thing is, in evaluating, you have to remember that he was immediately placed on the defensive. They made these wild, unfounded claims that "Russia is coming! Russia is coming!" They claimed Russia spent $100,000 on Facebook ads! Half of them for Trump and half of them for Hillary Clinton! Oh, that's going to change the world isn't it? My gosh, if that could determine the outcome of an election, you and I could go out and raise $100,000 and we could change the outcome of an election!

It was just so absurd. And here, they have investigated and run this thing down *ad nauseam* to where people are utterly sick of it. But it immediately put Trump on the defensive. They knew that if General Flynn didn't go, that we would have tensions go down and that meant a lot of people who deal in the oil markets could potentially lose a lot of money, people who run drugs across the border could lose money there. And, most of all, the most profitable of all vices is war, and if we didn't have war there were people who were going to lose untold billions of dollars.

Almost every major corporation profits from war, and so Michael Flynn had to go because he was the most dangerous person to their agenda. And then they continued to make these allegations and put Trump on the defensive to where Trump had to appear to be hostile towards Russia. If he seemed friendly, they'd say, "Aha! We told you that he really was going to normalize relations with Russia. He must be in their pocket." Well, no, he wasn't "in their pocket," he just recognized that it's better not to have a nuclear war.

The United States has been at war in the Middle East for seventeen years. That is longer than the First World War, the Second World War, and the Vietnam War combined. The grand total: We have been at war longer than the First World War, the Second World War and the Vietnam War combined. How long are we going to fight over there, and how can somebody demonstrate for you and for me one single thing that the people of the United States have ever gained from this? We've added seven trillion dollars to the national debt.

We made a big thing about how much President Obama added to the national debt. Fair enough. But nobody bothered to say, "Well, wait a minute. This wasn't all just his personal inclinations. Seven trillion dollars out of a $20-21 trillion debt is from these useless, stupid wars that we've fought." And anybody who says, "Well, we had to do it because we had to suppress terrorism,"—when we started off, the terrorists amounted to hundreds of people. Before we were finished, they were launching 20, 30, 40 mechanized armored divisions. They were taking over capitals of countries; they had expanded, controlling an area larger than many countries, and slaughtering hundreds and hundreds of thousands of people.

Where is the benefit? What have we achieved? Believe me; nobody loves our troops more than I do. I've been wounded in action. I volunteered over and over again for front line combat and I have tremendous respect for the guys who go over. They believe in their country, they believe in what we're doing. God bless them! My heart breaks for the ones who suffer. But we get the prosthetic devices, we get the caskets, while Saudi Arabia gets the oil money and Great Britain gets the empire. What do the American people get? What do we get out of all this stuff? Nothing!

Ripping up the Constitution

Wertz: Two events have just occurred and you have been addressing both of these. One was the raid, organized by Special Counsel Robert Mueller on the office and home of President Trump's personal attorney. Trump said this was an attack on the country and the values we stand for. He, again, called it a witch-hunt, and said that the client-lawyer privilege is dead. This raid is part of this entire British operation against the President which you've described, and occurs at the exact same time as the crisis in Syria. As you said, President Trump has been put in a defensive position: He's attacked for even calling President Putin and congratulating him on his election victory, for wanting to have a summit with Putin and good relations with Russia.

Michael Cohen, President Trump's attorney.

On the other hand, President Trump has been forced into a position where he says "I'm tougher on the Russians than my predecessor, Obama." He's being pressured to launch an attack, which is contrary to his own inclinations and contrary to the interests of the United States of America and of the world. And at the same time he comes under this attack from Mueller, which some people, including Alan Dershowitz, the attorney, who's a Democrat, are saying that this represents a dangerous day for American constitutional rights.

Black: This whole thing is a frontal attack on the U.S. Constitution. The Sixth Amendment to the Constitution guarantees people the right to counsel. The right to counsel, since the earliest days of the republic, has been assured by the idea of confidentiality. If you are going to have counsel, effective assistance of counsel, you have to share all of your information with them.

Alan Dershowitz is a Democrat. He has a reputation as a liberal Democrat from long ago. He was an Obama supporter, he was a Hillary supporter, but to his credit, he believes in the United States Constitution. He is absolutely distraught at what has happened. He said, "Where is the ACLU?" The ACLU would, he said, be screaming to high heaven, if this had this been a raid on the attorneys of Hillary Clinton, or Obama, or any other famous Democrat. You wouldn't be able to turn any radio or TV station without hearing somebody from the ACLU. It shows the very rapid erosion of the Constitution in the United States.

I think it is very dangerous, and who knows?—if they knew everything about you or me or any other American, they could find something that we have done. Years ago, back in the days of black and white TV, there was a TV show in which a bet was placed with a guy, the premise being, you'll get $10,000 if you don't commit a crime for one week. And the guy went for a week and they had him on the next week, and they said, "Well, it looks like you beat us." This is back in the days when people smoked. They then asked the guy, "What do you plan to do with all your money?" The host offers the guy a pack of cigarettes. The guy shuffles one out and lights up. The guy says, "Well, I might do this or that." And the host says, "I don't think so, because you just broke the law." The guy's jaw dropped, and he said, "What do you mean?" The host said "Federal law says that when you open a pack of cigarettes you have to break the stamp."

Everybody, no matter how diligent they are, everybody breaks laws, because we are a nation where almost everything is regulated, everything you do, and everything you say. They *know,* if they get into information that's held by Trump's attorney, there is something, there *is* something. We've got a special prosecutor, who does not feel constrained to find out certain things, and if they're not there, then dismiss it. The assault on the Sixth Amendment is the most blatant. I've been a lawyer since the 1970s, and I've never seen this happen before; a raid on an attorney's office and a fishing expedition to get at the client.

The Sixth Amendment is being torn down, just as the First Amendment has been torn down, the Fourth Amendment has been torn down, and the Tenth Amendment is gone. So much of what we grew up with as constitutional protections are destroyed. What is going on, with the search of Trump's records, is clearly unconstitutional in my view, and is immoral, and it is an attack on the Constitution.

Final Advice

Wertz: As we conclude, I would like to to give you an opportunity, perhaps, to address President Trump. What would you say to him now, in terms of the Syria situation, in particular, but more generally as well?

Black: I think I would tell him, "Look, there are certain areas where I can give you tremendous credit." Some of the economic things he's done I think have been very shrewd, very wise. The worst thing of all, though, is foreign policy. He has let foreign policy lead us to the brink of the third world war. His campaign promises *were exactly on point*. We don't really have any significant differences with Russia—I mean, not ones that are fundamental to the American national interest, except for stopping nuclear war.

That is the one national interest. NATO already spends four times as much as Russia does on its defense budget, and he's complaining they're not spending enough. Well, if four times isn't enough, how many times is? We need to diminish the role of NATO. Regime change needs to be absolutely out. Right now the United States has occupied, with our forces, a third of Syria, and we've done it secretly. Remember no boots on the ground? We've now got about 6,000 troops on the ground; a couple of them were killed just yesterday or the day before. We have a minimum of 12 American bases on sovereign Syrian territory. We're trying to redraw the map of Syria in a way that will *absolutely guarantee* the next war.

He should go back to what he said: We will work with Syria; we will end the war and do away with regime change. All of the things he campaigned on were great ideas, but I would give him a zero on foreign policy right now: I think it's very poor. He has surrounded himself with,—he always said I know how to pick the very best people. He has the worst war cabinet. At this point we look at General Mattis as being the dove of the bunch.

We've got Nikki Haley. She's supposed to be our top diplomat. You never hear her when she's not screaming hysterically for war. What kind of a diplomat is doing that? A dip-

U.S. Navy/Ronald Gutridge

Trident missile launched from an Ohio-class ballistic missile submarine.

lomat is supposed to be trying to find common ground, trying to move away from war. Nikki Haley, she's similar to John Bolton that way. If somebody says, "Let's attack Ireland," she'd say, "Yeah! Let's attack Ireland! Go after them! Kill them!" We've got to get away from this. We've got people who are really irrational.

Even Kushner, I think he's one of them, you know, even a member of Trump's family. I think it's a mistake to have so many family members around, the First Lady's fine. Everybody else can go and run the family business. He needs to surround himself with people who want to carry out his agenda. The people he has in foreign policy right now are people who are dead set against his agenda. That's what I would tell him: "You need somebody who believes in what you campaigned on, and that person needs to be your top advisor, not somebody like John Bolton who hated everything that you ever said on the campaign trail."

So that would be my advice. I'm not the President, unfortunately!

Wertz: I want to thank you very much for this interview.

Black: Thanks very much. It's always good to see you, Will. I appreciate all the things you're doing. It's groups like yours, and all of the individuals who go out and network with their friends on social media. Spread the film that you're going to put out on line, that's where our power lies. I wish you the best.

UN

Nikki Haley, U.S. Ambassador to the United Nations.

Wertz: Same to you.

Toward the Ecumenical Unity of East and West: Confucianism, Christianity, and the Peace of Faith

by Michael Billington

Adapted from a class presented by Michael Billington on March 31, 2018.

By putting the notion of the one mankind, defined from the standpoint of our common future as the reference point as how to think about political, economic, social, and cultural issues, President Xi has established a higher level of reason, a conceptual basis for a peace order on the whole planet. It is no coincidence that the concept for an entirely New Paradigm in human history would come from China, as it is coherent with the 2,500-year-old Confucian tradition.... Does this mean that the idea of building a harmonious world in which all nations can work together for the common aims of humanity is a utopia, a dream that can never become a reality? I believe that the universal history of mankind can provide the answer to that question, because it shows that there are some profound characteristics, the ideal of the highest humanity, shared by the most noble expressions of different cultures.

*—Helga Zepp-LaRouche,
to the Belt and Road Forum for
International Cooperation,
Beijing, May 14-15, 2017*

EIRNS

Michael Billington

The quote above, from Helga Zepp-LaRouche's speech at the Belt and Road conference in Beijing last year, is a very good introduction to the subject of this report. The previous classes in this series have presented the opposite poles within Western civilization—those of the Platonic tradition of a humanist conception that represents the recognition of the creative power of the human mind as the basis upon which all of humanity is defined; and counter to that, the oligarchical, Aristotelian idea that people are born either as masters or slaves, that people have to be governed in the same way animals are trained, with punishments and rewards and a strict hand, considering the mind is at best a kind of lifeless computer analyzing sense perceptions.

Such a world, as we've seen—especially as represented by the British Empire historically and the Aristotelian spokesmen for the British Empire, such as Hobbes, Locke, Hume, and Bertrand Russell—views man as an animal, justifying an oligarchical society. We've also seen that every great renaissance through-

Schiller Institute

Helga Zepp-LaRouche at the Belt and Road Forum for International Cooperation, May 14, 2017.

out our history, every great period of republican advance, was based on the opposite concept, that of the Platonic view of man, that man is born good through the creative power of the mind—the creative potential of every human being—to participate in the unfolding creation of the universe.

This is generally identified as a humanist Christian view in the West. Looking at that view from the perspective of another culture is most valuable. It's extremely important that everyone take into their heart a culture other than his or her own. At this point in history, looking at the incredible transformation in China and its contribution to the world through the New Silk Road, it's really almost the responsibility of every human being to look into Chinese history, Chinese culture, and Chinese philosophy. It's especially important since the spokesmen for the British Empire are terrified that the United States might actually link up with China, and with Russia. Lyndon LaRouche has argued for decades that the unity of these three great nations and cultures—and hopefully with India as well—is the necessary force needed to end the concept of Empire once and for all, to create a New Paradigm based on the common aims of mankind, as opposed to the British imperial view of the "lesser races" who have to be governed by the elite, by the aristocracy.

That would mean the end of the empire. We see that at hand now, and it's for that reason that we see such hysterical attacks on both China and Russia, and the demonization of Vladimir Putin and Xi Jinping. President Xi is declared to be a new Mao Zedong, a dictator who oppresses his people, who prevents freedom in his nation, who is an aggressor against his neighbors, and on and on, denying and covering up the greatest burst of creativity and invention seen in many decades, now taking place in China and expanding throughout the world through the New Silk Road.

For instance, Senator Marco Rubio and others in the Congress are trying to outlaw the Confucius Institutes, of which there are over one hundred in the United States, led by Chinese educators who have come to the United States, and to nations all over the world, to teach the Chinese language, culture and traditions. Marco Rubio declares that this language and cultural education is poisoning the minds of our children, making our children think that somehow there is something good in China when of course, we all should know that China is a dictatorial hell-hole, and so forth. It reminds me of the charges against Socrates—that he was poisoning the minds of the children through the Platonic approach to reason.

Creativity and Culture

It's generally the case that people in both the East and the West often accept the idea that there's some fundamental division between the Chinese way of thinking and the Western way of thinking, and that it's an unbridgeable gap. As Rudyard Kipling, the British imperialist said, "East is East and West is West, and never the twain shall meet." This is not a statement of fact, but a statement of British imperial policy, making sure that the division continues to exist. It is by keeping the world divided that imperial rule can be maintained over divided nations.

Of course, there are different characteristics to Western culture and Chinese culture. But those who argue that there are fundamental differences in ways of thinking, in the use of creative reason, are those who also argue that their side is the superior and the other side is inferior. You see this in China as well as you see it here.

What I want to do today is to refute that conception, to show that what is fundamental to human beings everywhere is this fight between the humanist conception of man and the oligarchical view of man as some sort of advanced animal at best; that this fight has existed in the entire history of Western culture and the entire history of Chinese culture; and in showing that, to show the compatibility between the humanist view on both sides and the common nature of the oligarchical view on both sides.

Look first at Gottfried Leibniz, who died in 1716. Leibniz was the seminal influence on the founders of the American republic. Leibniz was also a seminal influence on Lyndon LaRouche, in his teenage years when he was studying German critical philosophy and found that Leibniz had profound ideas that were coherent with his own sense of humanity. What might not be as well known is that Leibniz was also in very close collaboration with the Chinese. He was in correspondence with the Jesuit missionaries—this was the second group of Jesuit missionaries who had gone into China, many from Paris, where Leibniz was at that time. The missionaries were translating the works of Confucius, of Mencius, and especially of Zhu Xi, who is much less known in the West, but in a certain sense is comparable to Nicholas of Cusa, whose work gave rise to the Renaissance in Europe. In the 12th Century, during the Song Dynasty, Zhu Xi led a renaissance of Confucian thought, as Cusa had revived Platonic thought, and advanced it, in the West. There was a great renaissance in the Song dynasty, in science, art, philosophy and culture, which was only stopped by the Mongol invasion of China in the 13th Century that crushed much of Chinese civilization. Zhu Xi's ideas were later revived and remain the core of China's culture and system of government into modern times.

Leibniz studied the translations of the Chinese scholars intently. He recognized that there was a close similarity between the most fundamental Chinese philosophical ideas—what he called the "natural philosophy" or the "natural theology" of the Chinese—and those of Western Christian culture. He also recognized that the Chinese not only had great ideas, but had developed a nation which had far and away bigger cities than anything that existed in Europe at the time, a much more broadly educated population, and a highly developed educational system. Leibniz believed that one must look at long waves of history, and saw in China a culture that had succeeded in creating a highly advanced civilization, which civilization demonstrated that the Chinese must have discovered the most profound truths about man and nature. Only such discoveries could facilitate such a long-term development of an advanced culture.

Here is Leibniz, speaking of Eastern and Western culture:

> I consider it a singular plan of the fates that human cultivation and refinement should today be concentrated, as it were, in the two extremes of our continent, in Europe and in China, which adorns the Orient as Europe does the opposite edge of the Earth. Perhaps Supreme Providence has ordained such an arrangement, so that, as the most cultivated and distant peoples stretch out their arms to each other, those in between may gradually be brought to a better way of life.
>
> —*Novissima Sinica*, 1697

Gottfried Wilhelm Leibniz

Frontispiece of Novissima Sinica, *1697.*

This is a beautiful expression of what Helga Zepp-LaRouche calls "The Spirit of the New Silk Road." This is the concept that great civilizations, in coming in contact with each other, joining forces, acting on the basis of the common interests of these two cultures, can lift up the less developed portions of the world. This is precisely the concept that inspired Lyndon and Helga LaRouche when they first proposed the idea of the New Silk Road, following the collapse of the Soviet Union in the early 1990s.

To make it clear that we are always dealing with two opposite poles of thought, let me turn to the British Empire's Bertrand Russell, the man Lyndon LaRouche described as the "most evil person of the 20th Century." Not surprisingly, Bertrand Russell was also involved in China. At the time of World War I, Sun Yat Sen, the founder of the Chinese Republic in 1911, argued strenuously that China should stay out of the emerging war in Europe, which would become the First World War. But, he said, if we must be involved in the war, then we must be on the side of Germany, which was the least offensive of the colonial powers that had each grabbed a chunk of China during the previous hundred years. The British, Sun noted, had looted and destroyed; had imposed opium on the population and created mass famine; the Germans had been relatively more benevolent in Shandong, which was their sphere of influence in China. Sun said that if China were to join the war on the side of the British, and if the war was then won by the British, China would not share in the spoils. Rather, it would be chopped up and handed over to Japan and the other European powers. In fact, that's exactly what happened. Against his advice (he was not in power at the time), China joined with the British, playing a minor part in the war, and at the end of the war, China was indeed chopped up into little pieces. The German holdings were turned over to Japan, and other European countries took their share.

There arose an angry response against this by the Chinese people, led by the youth, called the May 4th Movement. In that movement, Sun Yat Sen was fighting to establish a republican concept, to bring his republican ideas to the fore in a revolutionary moment.

Unfortunately, on the other side, Bertrand Russell stuck his nose into it, along with John Dewey, his friend from the United States, who advocated "de-schooling," to "learn by doing" rather than through a classical education.

Together, Russell and Dewey helped create a radical anarchist faction within what later became the Communist Party of China. I would argue that it was at that time, under the influence of Russell and Dewey, that the ideas were born that ultimately came to the fore during the so-called Cultural Revolution from 1966-76—which was an absolute dark age for China, a period of self-destruction.

Here's what Bertrand Russell said in the book he wrote in 1922, called *The Problem of China*, after his extended time in China:

> Instinctive happiness, or the joy of life, is one of the most important … goods that we have lost through industrialism; its commonness in China is a strong reason for thinking well of Chinese civilization. Progress and efficiency, for example, make no appeal to the Chinese, except to those who have come under Western influence. By valuing progress and efficiency we have secured power and wealth; by ignoring them, the Chinese, until we brought disturbance, secured on the whole a peaceable existence and a life full of enjoyment.

This is a classic example of the "noble peasant" or "happy peasant" idea of British imperialism: Go into a country, profile it, find the most backward tendencies

Bertrand Russell, left, and his companion Dora Black on his arrival in Shanghai, China, in October 1920.

you possibly can, convince them that they are better off communing with nature, with a life expectancy of 22 or 23, while poisoning every aspect of an advanced culture that exists within that civilization. Especially in the case of China, you're dealing with a nation that had 5,000 years of one of the most advanced cultures in the world.

This is what you're dealing with still today, both in the West and in the East; the influence of Leibniz and the humanist conception, versus the British imperial conception, including empiricists like Russell who fundamentally hate human beings, who believe that you have to have masters and slaves, and of course, the masters must be British.

Confucianism

Confucius lived from 551 to 479 B.C. This is a poem he loved from the even more ancient *Book of Poetry*. It is one of the most simple and profound representations of Confucian thinking in all of the literature:

> Heaven, in creating Mankind,
> Created all things according to Law,
> Such that people can grasp these laws,
> And will love virtue.

This says many things. First of all, mankind was created. That's important. There are a lot of people who argue that Confucianism is not a religion, that it is not a faith, but just a philosophy. I don't think that is the important question, whether you call it a religion or not. Instead, address the Confucian concepts about man, nature, creativity and the creation of the universe. This poem states clearly: Mankind was created, it was not just some natural, arbitrary phenomenon, and by implication, the universe as a whole was created. By whom? The poem says, by Heaven—perhaps you could say God, but the Chinese say Heaven.

The next line says that Heaven created all things "according to Law," which means there is a lawfulness to that universe. It is not haphazard; it's not Darwinian survival of the fittest. There's a lawful development process that created all things, not only mankind, but nature itself, according to principles.

It goes on: The creation is intelligible, people can "grasp these laws." Lyndon LaRouche argues, similarly, that the basis for any scientific truth is that it can be subjected to an "intelligible representation"—that it is comprehensible to mankind, which can then put it into action through the creation of machine tools, applying them to the advancement of mankind.

The last line is the most important. Not only can people grasp these laws and apply them, but that will help them "love virtue." In other words, virtue is not just doing good or being kind, it's the advancement of human knowledge about the principles that exist in our universe, and applying those laws.

That, in a sense, encapsulates in my mind the entirety of the human tradition, East and West; and it's one which Confucius directly identified as the most profound concept. Mencius, later, quoted this poem and referenced the comments by Confucius, so it's clearly seen as a fundamental piece of their worldview.

Confucius

Natural Law and Civil Law

Look now at a quote from the encyclical *Rerum Novarum*, "On New Things," written by Pope Leo XIII in 1891. It addresses issues arising from the industrial revolution regarding relations between labor and capital, the rights of man in that new, changing society: "For laws are to be obeyed only insofar as they conform with right reason, and thus with the eternal laws of God."

This is a fundamental principle of the nation state. The fact that something is a law in a civil society does not mean that it's just, or even that it should be followed—a very revolutionary concept actually, and one which has been acted upon by people

Pope Leo XIII

of good will throughout history.

I would compare that with another famous saying of Confucius: "If there shall be distress and want within the Empire, the Mandate of Heaven shall be taken away from you forever."

The so-called "divine right of kings" existed at various times both in China and in Europe. There were tyrants who believed they were given the position as a mandate from Heaven, meaning that they had the right to effectively do whatever they wanted to do, that whatever they did was right because they were kings. Confucius, speaking to the king of one of the ancient kingdoms, said no—as the king you have the mandate of Heaven, but the mandate is that you have to make your society just and prosperous. And if, in fact, your policies have led to the general decay and collapse of your society, and people are in "distress and want," then that mandate of Heaven "shall be taken away from you forever." Again, a very revolutionary concept, and one which has been acted upon; and one which should prod us to action given the situation in the world today.

The Philosophy of *Ren*

Confucianism is generally known as the philosophy of *Ren* (sometimes spelled *Jen*). Here is what Confucius said when a student asked, what is *ren*? "Love all men," he answered. It's not just love. It's sometimes translated in English as "love." It's sometimes translated as "benevolence," but I would argue that the only accurate translation would be "*agapē*," which is the Greek word that has become commonly used in English as a higher form of love—a love of mankind as a whole, a love of God, a love of the Creation. In this passage, from the *Analects* of Confucius, the student then asks, "'What about wisdom?' The Master said, 'Know all men.'" It doesn't mean to know this or that fact, or to know every person in the universe, obviously. It means to know mankind, to know the nature of the human race.

Confucianism identifies Four Virtues. The first of these, and the greatest of these, is *Ren*, or *Agapē*. The others are Righteousness, Propriety (or the Rites, meaning right action, proper action which benefits oneself and society), and Wisdom (or Knowledge). Compare this with the very famous biblical passage from *I Corinthians* 13:13, which reads: "And now abideth faith, hope, and love (*agapē*), these three; but the greatest of these is love (*agapē*)."

The Greek word *agapē* is usually translated "charity" or "love" in this passage, but neither captures the original meaning of *agapē*. In fact, it is exactly parallel to the concept of *ren* in Chinese, meaning a higher form of love. Zhu Xi said that *ren* is the *principle* of love, or the *source* of love. This is the fundamental concept of Confucianism, with a very clear parallel in the Western humanist Christian tradition.

Mencius (372-289 B.C.)

The second great Confucian scholar, Mencius, lived almost two hundred years after Confucius. The book *Mencius*, a collection of his sayings and writings, is full of polemical criticisms of spokesmen of the several anti-Confucian sects, in which he addresses concepts of the mind and the nature of man in greater depth than his mentor Confucius. It makes for delightful reading.

Mencius

In the very first Book, Part 1, of *Mencius*, he says:

> They are only men of education, who, without a certain livelihood, are able to maintain a fixed heart. As to the people, if they have not a certain livelihood, it follows that they will not have a fixed heart. And if they have not a fixed heart, there is nothing which they will not do, in the way of self-abandonment, of moral deflection, of depravity, and of wild license. When they thus have been involved in crime, to follow them up and punish them—this is to entrap the people.

This is an elaboration on the concept of the Mandate of Heaven. If people don't have jobs, if they're unemployed, if they have no future, they are more likely to turn to drugs and crime and licentiousness. But then he adds that the government responsible for such conditions is more responsible than the criminal! You may need to arrest the criminal, but it is a form of entrapment!

In Book 6, Part 1, Mencius is talking to one of the kings:

> Is there any difference between killing a man with a stick and with a sword?
> The king said, "There is no difference!"
> Is there any difference between doing it with a sword and with the style of government?
> "There is no difference," was the reply.
> Then Mencius says,
> There are people dying from famine on the roads, and you do not issue the stores of your granaries for them. When people die, you say, "It is not owing to me; it is owing to the year [to the times]." In what does this differ from stabbing a man and killing him, and then saying—"It was not I; it was the weapon"? Let your Majesty cease to lay the blame on the year, and instantly from all the nation the people will come to you.

This is another expression of that idea of the mandate of Heaven.

Legalism

The primary political and ideological force which Mencius and his followers had to confront was that of Legalism, which became the foundation for the tyrannical rule of the so-called "First Emperor" in China, Qin Shi-Huang, who conquered the other kingdoms, consolidating China for the first time in 221 B.C. The two primary sources of Legalist thought were Xun Zi and Shang Yang.

Xun Zi said:

> The nature of man is evil; his goodness is acquired. Being what it is, man is born, first, with a

desire for gain.... Second, man is born with envy and hate.... Third man is born with passions of the ear and eye as well as the love of sound and beauty.

This doesn't mean the love of beauty in the profound sense, but rather avarice, wanting to hold and possess beautiful things. He basically asserts that man is an animal, just as an animal is not born with any of these natural qualities. He has to be trained the way an animal would be trained.

Shang Yang concurs, and applies that to politics, calling for the use of "the two handles"—punishment and reward: animal training, with "one reward for nine punishments." He also said: "If the ruler levies money from the rich in order to give alms to the poor, he is robbing the diligent and frugal and indulging the lazy and extravagant."

These were the thoughts that guided the Qin Shi-Huang dynasty. He believed that you were "guilty" if you were poor. Many of the poor were rounded up and sent out to do such things as building the wall. He began the first wall; not the wall you see today, but an earthen wall. The bodies of those who died building the wall were thrown into the wall itself. Chin Shi-Huang is most famous for having buried the Confucian scholars alive and for the burning of the Confucian books, some of which were lost to history.

The Qin Dynasty was overthrown only nineteen years later, giving rise to the Han Dynasty, which generally restored Confucian teaching, but in a manner similar to the Roman Empire at that time in the West, which adopted Christianity in name, but only as one among the many religions and multiple gods.

Mencius on the Mind

Mencius is most remembered for his insistence that man is born fundamentally good due to the creative powers of the mind. He said:

Benevolence (*ren*), righteousness, propriety, and knowledge are not infused into us from without. We are certainly furnished with them. And a different view is simply owing to want of reflection.

Shang Yang

Hence it is said, "Seek and you will find them. Neglect and you will lose them." Men differ from one another in regard to them—some as much again as others, some five times as much, and some to an incalculable amount—it is because they cannot carry out fully their natural powers.

He refers to these qualities as the "inborn luminous virtue," which exists within every human being as a potential. Because of the creative power of the mind, one has the potential to act upon these fundamental virtues. But, they tend to be obscured by the dependence on sense perceptions, by acting upon sense perceptions rather than the mind. On the mind, he says:

Therefore, if it receive its proper nourishment, there is nothing which will not grow. If it lose its proper nourishment, there is nothing which will not decay away. Confucius said, "Hold it fast, and it remains with you. Let it go, and you lose it. Its outgoing and incoming cannot be defined as to time or place." It is the mind of which this is said!

Mencius spoke directly about the notion of the sublime:

I like life, and I also like righteousness. If I cannot keep the two together, I will let life go, and choose righteousness. I like life indeed, but there is that which I like more than life, and therefore, I will not seek to possess it by any improper ways. I dislike death, indeed, but there is that which I dislike more than death, and therefore there are occasions when I will not avoid danger.

A reader today must surely be reminded of the famous speech by Martin Luther King on the night before he was assassinated, when he said that he had been to the mountaintop:

Like anybody, I would like to live a long life. Longevity has its place. But I'm not concerned about that now. I just want to do God's will. And He's allowed me to go up to the mountain. And I've looked over. And I've seen the Promised Land. I may not get there with you. But I want you to know tonight, that we, as a people, will get to the Promised Land!

This captures the profound notion of the sublime in man, the necessity that people look inside themselves for those qualities which are more important to them than life itself, for which they'd be willing to die. Not that they want to die, but that they would be willing, in order to achieve a greater purpose towards one's actual mission in life, which is eternal, which looks to the future of mankind. This was precisely the way that Mencius and later Zhu Xi thought.

One last quote from Mencius:

The disciple Gong Du said, "All are equally men, but some are great men, and some are little men—how is this?"

Mencius replied, "Those who follow that part of themselves which is great are great men; those who follow that part which is little are little men.

"The senses of hearing and seeing do not think, and are obscured by external things. To the mind belongs the office of thinking. By thinking, it gets the right view of things; by neglecting to think, it fails to do this. These—the senses and the mind—are what Heaven has given to us. Let a man first stand fast in the supremacy of the nobler part of his constitution, and the inferior part will not be able to take it from him. It is simply this which makes the great man."

Again here, it's this concept of the humanist creative powers of the mind versus sense perception, and against the political notion that the way to control people is through punishment and reward: rewards in the form of sensual pleasures like the pornography and the drugs and the violence and degradation that takes place today under the name of entertainment. This is titillating the senses in order to convince people that they need not think; that they can lead their lives in a way which has no long-term purpose, no goal either for oneself or for humanity as a whole.

Again, to show the contrast in China, I want to say a few words about Daoism, another anti-Confucian belief structure in ancient China, and one which is still influ-

Joseph Needham

ential today. Lao Zi, who lived about the same time as Confucius, is the primary figure of Daoism. He wrote the *Dao de Jing* (Classic of the Way), which is the favorite of British China-profilers and many in the counter-culture today. You can think of the Daoists as the Greenies of today, that we must not poison the Earth by developing technology. Lao Zi says:

Banish wisdom, discard knowledge and the
    people will be benefitted a hundredfold.
Banish benevolence, discard righteousness, and
    the people will be dutiful and compassionate.
Banish skill, discard profit, and thieves and
    robbers will disappear.
Banish learning, and there will be no more
    grieving.

The happy peasant! It is clear why the British imperialists and their cohorts love Daoism.

Here is a separate poem from Lao Zi. This was the favorite quote of Joseph Needham, who was the British Empire's China expert. His biography is called *The Man Who Loved China*, but the truth is he loved the backwardness of China. He wrote seventeen volumes called *The Science and Civilization of China*, but it is based on the lie that science in China came from this Daoist ideology. Joseph Needham loved the Cultural Revolution, praising the self-destruction of the nation as the pinnacle of Chinese greatness. Here is the poem of Lao Zi he so loved:

Heaven and Earth are without
benevolence [agapē].
They treat the ten thousand
things as straw dogs.
Nor is the sage benevolent
[agapic],
To him also are the hundred
clans but straw dogs.

The ten thousand things and the hundred clans are common ways of saying "all things" and "all people" in Chinese. Needham made no effort to hide his hatred for actual knowledge and actual humanity.

The other infamous Daoist was named Zhuang Zi, who lived several hundred years after Lao Zi. He often uses Confucius as a character in his stories, in an effort to ridicule and degrade him. One of the most famous describes Confucius walking along a country road, where he comes upon a peasant who is scooping water by hand out of a trench into his field, one scoop at a time. Confucius stops and says: "If you had a machine here, in a day you could irrigate one hundred times your present area. The labor required is trifling, as compared with the work done. Would you not like one?"

Confucius then describes a well-sweep—a machine like a mill-wheel, driven with foot-pedals, with multiple cups which scoop up water from the trench, transferring it into the field. Zhuang Zi then relates that this wise Daoist peasant denounces Confucius, saying that "anyone who is cunning with instruments must also have a scheming heart," and that the machine is "not a fit vehicle for the Dao." His last words: "It is not that I do not know of such things. I should be ashamed to use them."

Confucius and Schiller

One more comparison between East and West is drawn from Helga Zepp-LaRouche's lecture in New York on April 7 of this year, which beautifully compares the ideas of Confucius and the German poet Friedrich Schiller, after whom our Schiller Institute is named.

Schiller, in his essay "Grace and Dignity," defines what he calls the "beautiful soul" or the "golden soul" in this way:

Friedrich Schiller

We call it the beautiful soul when the moral sentiment has assured itself of all emotions of a person, ultimately to the degree that it may abandon the guidance of the will to emotions, and never run the danger of being in contradiction with its own decisions.

It is often debated whether one should favor the mind over emotions, or the other way around. But, Schiller—and as you'll see also in Confucius and other Confucians—made the point that one must not suppress the emotions, but uplift them, to the level of the creative mind. This is what Leibniz meant when he talked about happiness, as in the U.S. Constitutional commitment to "life, liberty, and the pursuit of happiness," which comes from Leibniz. He certainly didn't mean the happiness of the flesh, but that happiness which comes from participating in developing or mastering great discoveries in science, classical music and art, from knowing that you are contributing in a way that is going to advance all of mankind, by contributing new knowledge and new artistic beauty to the universe.

Schiller is saying the same thing. You have to lift those emotions up to the point where they are so committed to beauty and to the Good that you can follow your emotions, because you trust that they are not going to lead you to do anything against the Good. This is what Schiller meant by the beautiful soul.

Confucius had a very similar concept, which is seen in this famous section from the *Analects*. In a sense, he's describing his own progress through life, but really he's talking about the stages that people should go through in self-development:

At 15 I set my heart on learning; [He'd reached puberty and he began serious study. By 15, LaRouche was already a committed Leibnizian.]

At 30 I firmly took my stand; [This is particularly important. When the Red Army took over China in 1949, Mao Zedong, standing in Tiananmen Square, before the throng, said "China has stood up." Everyone knew that this was a reference to this idea in Confucius—the nation had reached adulthood, and could begin the productive part of its life.]

At 40 I had no delusions;

At 50 I knew the mandate of heaven;

At 60 my ear was attuned; [And here he means the senses were attuned to beauty.]

At 70 I could follow my heart's desire without overstepping the boundaries.

This final line is precisely the same as Schiller's idea. By 70, he had so ennobled his emotions, "my heart's desire," that he could follow them, fully trusting that he would not do anything against his mission in life, his sense of duty and responsibility and mission.

Zhu Xi and the Confucian Renaissance

We come now to the genius Zhu Xi, and I believe this is the core of what must be understood in the West to gain a sense of what the Confucian renaissance was about in the Song Dynasty in the 12th Century, and the renaissance taking place today in China.

Zhu Xi lived from 1130 to 1200. He was among those known as neo-Confucians, although I don't like the term neo-Confucians, since philosophers with totally different ideas are grouped together under that term. I think it's better to say that he

Zhu Xi

and his circle initiated a Confucian renaissance. I will compare his work to that of Nicholas of Cusa, the key figure in launching the Renaissance in Europe in the 15th Century.

First, read the following section of Lyndon La-Rouche's Preface to his *The Science of Christian Economy*, one of his prison writings published in 1991. He begins by quoting from the encyclical *Rerum Novarum* by Pope Leo XIII in 1891, referenced above: "For laws are to be obeyed only insofar as they conform with right reason and thus with the eternal law of God."

LaRouche then references the decay of modern so-ciety, referring to the "New Age" of the "rock-drug-sex counter culture and increasingly irrational, mass-murderous expressions of self-styled 'ecologism,' or 'neo-Malthusianism'." He continues:

What is notable on these accounts is the increasingly emboldened way in which the two evils, the "New Age" and usury, have exhibited their natural affinities for one another, combining their forces in even the highest places of Anglo-American power, to demand, in the misused name of "freedom" and "ecology," the rapid extermination and global outlawing of every scientific and moral barrier which has hitherto existed as impediments to rampaging immiseration and dictatorial oppression of mankind....

We propose that it is necessary, but not sufficient to view the referenced state of affairs from a Christian standpoint; for practical reasons, it is essential that even the Christian standpoint itself be presented here from an ecumenical standpoint as *ecumenical* is typified by Cardinal Nicholas of Cusa's dialogue, his *De Pace Fidei* (On the Peace of Faith).

Different faiths, religious and/or secularist, can be brought to principled agreement only in two possible alternate ways of manifesting mutual good will. In the one case, they may agree on a common point of taught doctrine, such as the principle of monotheism, as in opposition to the pantheistic pluralism of pagan Babylon, Rome, or the Apollo Cult at Delphi. Or, otherwise, differing faiths may reach coincidence of principled views by the means indicated in the referenced features of the encyclical [of Pope Leo XIII] ... It is the latter alternative upon which we concentrate attention here.

Faith may read those writings it deems sacred, or as authoritative commentaries on such writings. Or, faith may "read the bare book of universal nature," a book which plainly has been written directly by none other than the Creator himself. It is certain to all men and women of ecumenical good will, that the two kinds of books—the written ones, and the book of nature—cannot contradict one another, on condition that the written one be true, and that both the written and the natural one be read by means of the inner eye of true reason.

So, where doctrinal writings differ, we may turn the eye of ecumenical reason to the common book of nature. Let us argue the point in the following, twofold way. We emphasize, on the one side, the ecumenical notion of *intelligible representation* of a principle of knowledge of cause-effect in our universe, a means by which all men and women, despite differences in profession of monotheistic faith, may be brought by their own powers of reason to agreement upon a common principle of law. Second, we emphasize the importance of stressing *Christian* principles of Christian civilization as *Christian*, even within the framework of a monotheistic ecumenicism.

Consider next this simple illustration. The most ancient among known astronomies, that of the ancient Vedic peoples of Central Asia, illustrates the obvious manner in which a so-called "primitive" people may construct a reliable solar astronomical calendar from scratch. Observe successively the position of the Sun, at dawn, mid-day, and sunset. Mark these observations each in stone. At night, observe the constellations and their stars, to which each of the respective three, day-time observations point. After five years, we have thus the data on which to base a solar astronomical calendar of approximately 365 days per calendar year, measuring the year either from the winter solstice to winter solstice or from the vernal equinox to vernal equinox.

By the same method, the long decimillennial equinoctial cycle is adduced. So, a system of solar astronomy, free of the whore-goddesses Shakti's and Ishtar's lunacies, is built up by aid of reason. So the book of nature may be read. God's book of nature. In such successive revolutions, and related ways, *reason* reveals to us that our universe has the apparent form of a unified cause-effect process of *Becoming*, a process of *Becoming* which is subsumed by an indivisible Supreme Being, who embodies, among other qualities, what Plato admired as the *Good*. Of such matters of principle, in such a manner, do the very stones cry out.

Consequently, when we demonstrate by access to reason that a certain universal or approximately universal principle must be true, a monotheistic ecumenicism has gained a two-fold advantage. Since all of human knowledge is finally supplied by reason, there can be no valid teaching presented by any religion which contradicts true reason, as we define *reason* in the following chapters; there can be no valid objection to this principle which is to be tolerated on premise of secularist rejection of religious precept.

Now we can look at Zhu Xi and Cusa. Zhu Xi's school is called the School of Principle. The word for principle is *Li*. The idea of principle, this concept of *Li*, was not a major concept in Confucius' and Mencius' writings; it's something which Zhu Xi gave a special meaning to in further developing the Confucian understanding. Zhu Xi distinguishes between Universal Principle, which is the principle of the universe as a whole, and the individual Principle which is inherent in all created things. He writes: "Universal Principle is simply a comprehensive term for the four virtues [*ren*, righteousness, propriety, and wisdom], and each of them is an individual enumeration for Universal Principle."

The virtues are themselves expressions of the totality of the Universal Principle.

Leibniz, as I said, had studied the writings of Zhu Xi extensively, as well as those of Confucius and Mencius. Here's what he says about this concept of the *Li*, the principle. This is in his *Novissima Sinica*:

The first principle of the Chinese is called *Li*, that is, Reason, or the foundation of all nature, the most universal reason and substance; there is nothing greater nor better than *Li*. . . . [It] is not at all capable of divisibility as regards its being, and is the principal basis of all the essences which are and which can exist in the world. But it is also the aggregation of the most perfect multiplicity because the Being of this principle contains the essences of things as they are in their germinal state. We say as much when we teach that the ideas, the primitive grounds, the prototypes of all essences are all in God.... The Chinese also attribute to the *Li* all manner of perfection ... so perfect that there is nothing to add. One has said it all. Consequently, can we not say that the *Li* of the Chinese is the sovereign substance which we revere under the name of God?

Note the expression: "the Being of this principle contains the essences of things as they are in their germinal state." Leibniz had his own theory called the *Monadology*, which basically expresses the concept that the monad of the universe as a whole subsumes the essence of every created thing—the multiplicity of things, of individual monads—while each individual monad is a reflection of the totality. This is very close to Zhu Xi's concept of *Li*.

Let's look closely at the next passage, known as "The Great Learning," or *Daxue* in Chinese. *Da* means big or great, and *Xue* means to study or scholarship. The term was generally interpreted within China as "The Great Learning," but Zhu Xi actually gave it a different interpretation: He said that it should rather be interpreted as "Learning for Adults," where the *Da* means adults, grown-ups, and *xue* means learning.

Zhu Xi did something quite extraordinary in his interpretation of the entire *Daxue*. Read first of all how "The Great Learning" was interpreted in the traditional way:

The ancients who wished to illustrate illustrious virtue throughout the kingdom, first ordered well their own states. Wishing to order well their states, they first regulated their families. Wishing to regulate their families, they first cultivated their persons. Wishing to cultivate their persons, they first rectified their hearts. Wishing to rectify their hearts, they first sought to be sincere in their thoughts. Wishing to be sincere in their thoughts, they first extended to the utmost their knowledge. Such extension of knowledge lay in the investigation of things.

Now, this has good qualities to it, but Zhu Xi said this is not what Confucius meant. Look at the first sentence—it is appealing to the king, to "illustrate illustrious virtue" to the people. But Zhu Xi said that the true meaning is for *all* people to "illustrate illustrious virtue," not only the king. So Zhu Xi interpreted the first sentence to be: "Those of antiquity who wished that all men throughout the empire keep their inborn luminous virtue unobscured, put governing their states well first."

So Zhu Xi said, basically, Confucius didn't mean this is only for the king—this great learning is not only for the leaders, it's for all people. Not only that all people must be encouraged to live up to their "inborn luminous virtue," but also that all people must know that they have the capability, as human beings, to express this inborn luminous virtue, which you don't want to obscure by the influence of sensual perceptions which disrupt the mind.

Also, at the end of Zhu Xi's first sentence, he says that *all* men throughout the empire "put governing their states well first." So, governing the state is also not just the responsibility of the king. Governing the state is the responsibility of all men. In other words, he is universalizing this as a principle of humanity.

Zhu Xi also changes the final sentence in the traditional interpretation, which said that "extension of knowledge lay in the investigation of things." But, Zhu Xi says, this should be interpreted: "The extension of knowledge lies in fully apprehending *the principle in things*."

Think about that. We've already shown that he believed that there was a fundamental principle to all created things, which was not a sensual facet, but a principle which connected it to the Universal Principle. As in Plato's cave analogy, the things one sees with the senses are only a reflection of its principle, its essence. The physical existence is a shadow of a more profound existence, how it came to be as part of the unfolding creation, and what its role is in the unfolding creation. This is what Lyndon LaRouche calls the "Becoming"—what its role is in that creative process, with man being the most advanced form of that because of the human mind.

So, Zhu Xi says that "The extension of knowledge lies in fully apprehending the principle in things." You can't understand the principle in something by measuring it, or touching it, or smelling it, or tasting it. To understand the principle in things, you first of all have to start from the universe as a whole, the way Kepler did when he was examining the Solar system. He came up with laws for the Solar system because he began with a principle, that in fact the Solar system must have coherence with other aspects of the creation—the musical scale, for instance, which he knew was something man had discovered—concepts which man had discovered as existing in the physical universe, but had not been known until man discovered them.

In that sense, you have to start from a universal principle, and you have to examine things—actions, people, and physical objects—from the question of their role in the unfolding creation of the universe. This is a much higher conception of the creation.

Zhu Xi had his opponents, who didn't agree with him on this. They didn't like the idea that he thought he could go back and change "the way things were."

Nicholas of Cusa

Now look at Nicholas of Cusa's essay *De Pace Fidei* (On the Peace of Faith), as translated by Will Wertz. Cusa was basically arguing, as La-Rouche indicated above, that you can find a fundamental truth within any and all monotheistic religions, and that you can thereby come to an ecumenical agreement among religions as a way of maintaining peace, if they can convince each other, and themselves, that there is in fact one unified, universal grain of truth in any monotheistic conception of the universe.

Cusa portrays a dialogue between God, the Word, with a Roman Catholic, an Orthodox Christian, a Jew, a Muslim, and a few others. In the debate, he presents the idea of the Trinity as understood in Christianity as something which could be understood, not in terms of the Christian concept of God the Father, God the Son, and God the Holy Spirit, but rather, in terms of principles of nature—as LaRouche said, "The stones cry out"—that you can find an intelligible representation which is a universal expression of what in Christianity is called the Trinity.

The Word addresses the gathered wise men about their various faiths:

> You will not find another faith, but rather one and the same single religion presupposed everywhere. You, who are now present here, are called wise men by the sharers of your language, or at the very least philosophers or lovers of wisdom.

Nicholas of Cusa
1401-1464

There can only be one wisdom.... Prior to every creature there is wisdom through which everything created is that which it is.

The Word gains their agreement on that point, and then defines a three-fold nature of the universe. He says there is an overall principle of wisdom—we could call it Unity, because it is completely combined, it's indivisible. And yet, enfolded in that Unity is all the multiplicity of created things. Those things are Equal in the sense that they're all participating in an unfolding creation—participating in the "Becoming." That is their Equality, an Equality in the Unity of the created universe. And, the Connection between this Equality and the Unity is the principle of *agapē*; a higher sense of love, or you could say, of creativity.

Thus, Cusa reasons, there is this universal way of expressing the Trinity: the Unity, the Equality, and the Connection of all things. The Word says later, "Some name Unity Father, Equality Son, and Connection the Holy Spirit, since those designations, even though they are not proper, nevertheless suitably designate the Trinity." Cusa is asserting that this scientific way of looking at it is actually a higher conception, in order to show the triune nature of the unfolding creativity of the universe. It forces you not to have a fixed sense of nature as a finished product, or of God as an exterior thing. There's a connection, an equality of all things through the participation in this lawful unity of the expanding universe.

Then, just below the "Three-fold nature: Unity, Equality, and Connection," Cusa says there can also be only one Eternal:

> However, there cannot be several eternals. Consequently, in the one eternity is found unity, equality of unity, and the union of unity and equality, or connection. Thus, the most simple origin of the universe is triune, since in the origin the originated must be enfolded. Everything originated, however, signifies that it is thus enfolded in its origin, and in everything originated a three-

fold distinction of this kind can be found in the unity of the essence. And for this reason, the simplest origin of everything will be three and one.

The Confucian Trinity

What I was doing, in my work in prison, was to extend Cusa's work to embrace Confucianism. Cusa did not know about Confucius, so there was no Confucian in the dialogue *On the Peace of Faith*. My conclusion should be clear from the above.

If you want to think of a Confucian trinity of Unity, Equality, and Connection, I have defined it here as:

• Universal *Li*, the Universal Principle, which Leibniz compared to the Christian notion of God, the origin of the universe and the Unity of the universe;

• Individual *Li*, the principle of each created thing; the nature of every created thing as it reflects Equality with the Universal;

• *Ren*, as I have equated *ren* with *agapē*, which connects the principle of all created things to the universal principle.

I will close this discussion with the primary example of the opposition to Zhu Xi, that of Wang Yang Ming, who lived a couple of hundred years after Zhu Xi, and whom many unfortunately link with Zhu Xi as a fellow Neo-Confucian. Wang Yang Ming called himself a Confucian, but he is an Aristotelian who became more identified with the Daoist ideology and Zen Buddhist ideology than with Confucianism. His refutation of Zhu Xi is comical but revealing.

Wang decided to test Zhu Xi's hypothesis that every created thing possessed an essence, a principle. He and a friend therefore sat down in his father's garden in front of some bamboo, and determined to sit there and study this bamboo until they discovered the principle of bamboo. They sat there for many hours until they finally got sick and had to give up. His conclusion: There's no such thing as principle; it doesn't exist. It's only what's in your mind; that's the only thing that's real to Wang Yang Ming. Cultural relativism, basically.

Sun Yat Sen

Sun Yat Sen

I will not address here all of the rich contributions of Sun Yat Sen, the leader of the Republican revolution in China in 1911, but I want to conclude with a note about his view of Confucianism. Sun was educated in the American System by an American family in Hawaii, where he had gone to work and study in the 1880s, and became a dedicated advocate of the Hamiltonian concepts of political economy.

He became a Christian, but remained a Confucian. He said: "We must revive not only our old morality, but also our old learning …, the Great Learning," the *Daxue* that I discussed above. He then essentially paraphrased the *Daxue*:

Search into the nature of things [notice he doesn't say "investigate things," but "Search into the nature of things," the principle underlying existence], extend the boundaries of knowledge, make the purpose sincere, regulate the mind, cultivate personal virtue, rule the family, govern the state, pacify the world.

Of course, "pacify the world" is not in the *Daxue,* which was only addressing China. But Sun Yat Sen universalized that concept, saying that the last step in this progression is to "pacify the world."

Sun Yat Sen said later, "Let us pledge ourselves to lift up the fallen and to aid the weak; then, when we become strong and look back upon our own sufferings under the political and economic domination of the Powers, and see weaker and smaller peoples undergoing similar treatment, we will rise and smite that imperialism. Then will we be truly governing the state and pacifying the world." Thus, he saw it to be a Confucian responsibility for China to rise and bring about development in the world, unlike the imperialist looting that had dominated the era of the European powers.

This is indeed a description of what Xi Jinping is doing today through the New Silk Road.

Chinese President at Boao Announces New Phase of Reform and Opening Up

by William Jones

April 15—The annual Boao Forum, held on the southern Chinese island of Hainan, April 8-11, which has gathered together leaders from Asia since its inception in 2001, has always attracted interest far beyond the Asia-Pacific region. Boao was established by a number of the Asian countries in the aftermath of the 1997 Asia financial crisis, in an attempt to find Asian solutions to Asian problems. Each year Boao brings together business and political leaders from all over the world to discuss the economic agenda and plan for the future. The growing role of China in the world economy has now made the Boao Forum a focus of intense international interest. And

The Boao Forum for Asia, April 2018.

with the historic 19th Party Congress last year, and the National People's Congress this year, China has embarked on a new era in its reform and opening up policy, which has tremendous implications for the region and the world, and which has been closely watched by business leaders around the world.

The keynote speech of Chinese President Xi Jinping at this particular gathering was therefore awaited with great expectation by the participants and by the world. And they were not to be disappointed.

Speaking on April 10, President Xi gave a broad sweep of China's development since the "reform and opening up" launched by Deng Xiaoping 40 years ago this year. Xi pointed in particular to the development of Hainan Island, where the conference was located, as an example of the progress made during that period. The reform and opening up, Xi said, had transformed Hainan "from the once backward and remote island

into one of China's most open and dynamic regions." Hainan is celebrating its 30th anniversary as one of the 16 Special Economic Zones established as a part of the reform and opening up. And Xi's comments on Hainan's development presaged the plans that he would announce a few days later that China intended to make Hainan the country's first international free trade port since the founding of the People's Republic.

The "reform and opening up" had made the rapid development of the Chinese economy possible and had transformed China into the most important locomotive of global economic development. "Over the last four decades," Xi said, "the Chinese people have significantly unleashed and enhanced productivity in China through hard work with an unyielding spirit. Heaven rewards those who work hard, and flowers in spring come to fruition in autumn. The focused endeavor in national development and unwavering commitment to reform and opening-up of the Chinese people have brought enormous changes to the country."

This process was never easy and suffered its reverses and reformulations throughout that period. Initially it was thought by most Western observers, and indeed, even some Chinese observers, that China would somehow "morph into" just another G7 or G8 member and adopt "Western norms and habits of thought." Much of this was based on a lack of understanding of China and its culture, and the struggle which had led to the entry of the People's Republic of China into the circle of major powers. In addition, the 2008 financial crisis made it clear to the Chinese, and the world, that the Western norms and habits were not terribly conducive to rapid economic development, particularly in the developing world.

How China Sees Its Mission

These Western expectations also ignored the strong commitment that China had to its socialist heritage. "Over the last four decades, the Chinese people have kept forging ahead and demonstrated the strength of the nation through keeping pace with the progress of the times," Xi said. "Ours is a truth-seeking nation with an open mind. Our efforts to open up our minds have advanced side by side with our endeavor of reform and opening-up. Our search for new ideas and experiment of practices have been mutually reinforcing. Such is the great strength of a guiding vision. Ours is a nation that has courageously engaged in self-revolution and self-reform, constantly made improvements to the system of socialism with Chinese characteristics, and kept overcoming institutional and systematic obstacles to development."

The mistaken expectations also ignored the fact that China would not simply "take its place" among the major industrial powers. It was also committed to advancing the needs of the other countries which were suffering extreme poverty and underdevelopment and with whom China maintained strong bonds of solidarity. Through the Belt and Road Initiative and the new model of international relations based on win-win cooperation that China has put forward, it has created a model in which no country will be left behind.

"The world is undergoing a new round of major development, great change and profound readjustment," Xi said. "Humankind still faces many instabilities and uncertainties. The new round of technological and industrial revolution brings fresh opportunities

Xinhua/Li Xueren

Chinese President Xi Jinping delivering keynote speech at the Boao Forum.

and presents unprecedented challenges. In some countries and regions, people are still living in the shadow of war and conflict. A great many people, including the old, women, and children, are suffering from hunger and poverty. Climate change and major communicable diseases remain formidable challenges. Humanity has a major choice to make between openness and isolation, and between progress and retrogression."

And China is intent that the opening up will continue and be taken to a higher level. China has made remarkable gains in various areas of science and technology, becoming the leader in a number of fields and making unique breakthroughs in a number of scientific areas, and has benefited greatly from its access to the world around it. The native talent of the Chinese people, combined with the gains made in technology worldwide during the last few decades, have led to major breakthroughs by Chinese researchers in many areas of human endeavor. And it was with the help of these breakthroughs that China has been able to lift over 700 million from poverty during that process. Only through an expansion of that important collaboration between East and West can China to move its mode of production to "high-quality" development and innovation.

China-U.S. Cooperation Will Be a Signal

Xi stressed that China would continue to facilitate investment in China by foreign corporations, assuring that even up to 51% ownership in some areas, a majority interest, would be available, and that China would also open up new economic areas for foreign investment, including in finance and insurance. China would also strengthen legislation to protect intellectual property rights for Chinese as well as foreign enterprises, and would not require technology transfers from firms wishing to invest in China. President Xi in this way addressed most of the trade concerns which President Trump had raised as the reason for his tariff threat.

While most of these measures had already been laid out in the work report of Premier Li Keqiang at the National Peoples Congress last month and by President Xi in his wide-ranging final

Xinhua/Yao Dawei

Meeting between Chinese President Xi Jinping and former President of Kyrgyzstan, Almazbek Atambayev, during the Boao Forum.

speech to the Congress, the emphasis by the Chinese President at such an international forum as Boao gave it even added emphasis. And, in the context of the growing trade problems with the U.S., it was also seen as an olive branch to bring the process back to negotiations and away from threats. The initial positive response by President Trump to Xi's speech in a tweet gives a good indication that this message has been received, and might help avert the threat of any trade war.

Xi also laid out the path China would follow in this new phase of development. "Following the people-centered development philosophy and the new development vision, we will modernize our economic system, deepen the supply-side structural reform, and implement at a faster pace the strategies of innovation-driven development, rural revitalization and coordinated regional development," Xi said. "We will continue to work on targeted poverty alleviation and promote social equity and justice to give our people a greater sense of fulfillment, happiness, and security."

At the same time, President Xi clearly delineated his proposal for a new development model for the world, a model that is inclusive and based on the concept of mutual benefit and win-win cooperation. "We live at a time with an overwhelming trend toward peace and cooperation," Xi said.

"In a world aspiring for peace and development, the Cold-War and zero-sum mentality looks even more out of place. Putting oneself on a pedestal or trying to immunize oneself from adverse developments will get nowhere. Only peaceful development and cooperation can truly bring win-win or all-win results. We live at a time with an overwhelming trend toward openness and connectivity. Human history shows that openness leads to progress while seclusion leaves one behind. The world has become a global village where our interests are intertwined and our economic and social progress interconnected. To promote common prosperity and development in today's world, we have no choice but to pursue greater connectivity and integrated development."

Xi's vision of this new model of international relations has received strong support from all over the world. Almost 100 countries have expressed support for Xi's Belt and Road Initiative. Xi's concept of a "community of a shared future for mankind" has been enshrined in documents of the United Nations, and the presence at Boao of the Austrian President and the Netherlands Prime Minister further underlined the important influence China is having on the Western nations as well. It is hoped that the U.S. President, who has heard Xi Jinping's proposals at Boao on China's reform path, will also hear and understand the implications of the Chinese President's broader proposal. If China and the United States can work together on a win-win basis, this signal will be heard around the world.

April 9: Music at the Service of Truth Alone

by Dennis Speed

April 16—"Slavery of the body, and slavery of the soul, are two very different things. Sometime slaves are kings, and kings are really slaves. Sometimes slaves can change not only their names, but their destiny, and even all of history. If one man, born a slave, is sovereign over the power of his own mind, he can free a whole people."

Thus did actor Ed Asner's first words, delivered in his narration of *From the Mountaintop: A Concert Commemorating the Life of Dr. Martin Luther King*, announce not only the theme, but the purpose of the evening's musical-pedagogical exercise. Classical Music as a weapon for the aesthetic education of mankind; the use of the Classical chorus in tragedy; and the particular role of the Schiller Institute's New York City Chorus in changing the tragic axioms of popular opinion, to avert the presently unfolding world-tragedy— these were the pressing, persisting questions deemed urgent and essential to discuss with a Manhattan audience on the April 9, 50th anniversary of King's 1968 funeral.

The concert, in which the Schiller Institute chorus played a prominent role, was performed two days after the Schiller Institute conference, "Bending the Arc of the Moral Universe Toward Economic Justice," addressed by Helga Zepp-LaRouche. That conference also featured a presentation by Jason Ross, co-author of the Schiller Institute report, "Extending the New Silk Road to Southwest Asia and Africa." In response to a questioner, Zepp-LaRouche said:

And since we have this event today, because of the 50th anniversary of the assassination of Martin Luther King, I think it's a very good moment in history, to say, we will not allow the murderers of King to be successful in eliminating the hope which he represented. Martin Luther King was murdered at a moment when he had started to pick up many of the same issues which are now being, in reality, changed by China. Because he had started not only to take up the question of economic justice *inside* the

New York Schiller Institute Chorus at April 9 concert commemorating Martin Luther King.

United States, but also he had started to take on the question of jobs and overcoming poverty in developing countries. And that is what China is doing, exactly today. In the same way, what the Schiller Institute has been campaigning for, and LaRouche and his movement have been working for, for almost half a century, is now becoming a reality.

So there is reason for optimism. And I think that the best thing we can do in a moment like this, thinking about the memory of Martin Luther King, is to say, we will pick up the torch, we will not allow the American people to be passive and desperate and ignorant and all of these things, but we will all turn into active members of the Schiller Institute, help to spread the message; make the Schiller Institute a Renaissance movement, a moment fighting not only for the economic buildup of the United States, but also for a cultural Renaissance. I think the two things absolutely have to go together.

cc/Abernathy Family Photos

March 1965 Montgomery to Selma march. Dr. and Mrs. Martin Luther King, center, and Dr. Ralph Abernathy, far left with hat, and Abernathy's three children in the front.

These remarks, and the Zepp-LaRouche speech, anticipated the unexpected events that would confront those in attendance at the concert, and all Americans and world-citizens, only hours later. Most in that Monday audience could not have earlier known that the world would be on the verge of a potential thermonuclear war as that evening's performance would begin.

A statement on behalf of Zepp-LaRouche to the 700-person audience read: "As you are assembled tonight, in the last hours, the danger of war, even thermonuclear war, has increased. The United Nations has been meeting to discuss Syria. The very existence of world civilization hangs on whether the world's leaders, in China, Russia and the United States, in particular, now, together, find a way out of the old paradigm of war and geopolitics."

Rev. Bernard Lafayette, chairman of the National Board of Dr. King's Southern Christian Leadership Conference and a long-time associate of Dr. King, also presented a message to the assembled audience: "Whether it is North Korea or North Vietnam, America has no intrinsic enemies that cannot be addressed through dialogue. We need a bridge to China, a bridge to Russia, and we need to remember what John Kennedy said: 'Mankind will put an end to war, or war will put an end to mankind.' Mankind has to wage peace, rather than wage war." His remarks were delivered by Andrea King, a graduate of Lafayette's nonviolence training and a member of the St. Batholomew's Church where the concert was held. (Dr. Lafayette was unable to attend because of a last-minute scheduling conflict.)

Singing Awake America's Conscience

On April 4, 1967, Martin Luther King had stunned the world, including his life-long supporters, with his Riverside Church speech, "Time to Break the Silence," declaring on that occasion his staunch, fully considered, and thorough-composed opposition to the war in Southeast Asia. He had famously declared, "The choice today is no longer between violence and nonviolence; it's nonviolence or nonexistence," referring to thermonuclear weapons and the continuation of hostile relations with Russia, then the Soviet Union. One year later to the day, he was dead. The night before his death, however, he had given one of the most powerful, and perhaps the most prescient of orations in American history.

It was to musically frame those final words of that

speech, "I've been to the mountaintop…. Mine eyes have seen the glory of the coming of the Lord!" that the ordering and placement of the musical and narrative selections of the concert itself were devoted. All of the musical action moved toward, and then away from, King's "Gethsemane moment," the evening of April 3, 1968, when he proudly and defiantly announced, over the course of a twenty-five minute speech, to an audience of 2,000 sanitation workers and their supporters serving as witnesses, his intention to "stay on the mountaintop" despite the threats to his life. The following is an excerpt from the concert program about Martin Luther King's nearly completely extemporaneous speech:

The poem would never have been made, would never have been composed and declaimed, except for the determined intervention of the Rev. Ralph Abernathy, Martin Luther King's closest friend. Abernathy, who, in his introduction to King that night, would humorously refer to himself as "[King's] dearest friend and other brother," had brought King there, despite his fatigue and reluctance to appear.

The author Taylor Branch reports what came next: "Abernathy told King this was a core crowd of sanitation workers who had braved a night of hell-fire to hear him, and they would feel cut off from a lifeline if he let them down. His entrance caused an eerie bedlam…. Cheers from the floor echoed around the thousands of empty seats above, and the whole structure rattled from the pounding elements of wind, thunder, and rain…. King came smiling to the microphones about 9:30 p.m., just as the storms crested."

Outside, "the wind howled like a hammer." There were multiple tornadoes; at least five people died. Rain fell in slanted sheets, and only about two thousand people were there that night in Bishop Charles Mason Temple, unlike the 15,000 that had heard King there two weeks before. King was at the lowest ebb of his popularity in his entire career; 75 percent of the nation's population thought he had lost touch with the American people, particularly because of his

Library of Congress/Warren Leffler

Dr. Ralph David Abernathy

announced opposition to the Vietnam War. The sanitation workers, prevented from forming a union, were on strike because of the deaths of Echol Cole and Robert Walker. They had both been crushed to death on the previous Feb. 1 by a malfunctioning compactor in their truck, forced by rain to sit in the truck's garbage bay because, under segregation, they were legally prohibited from seeking shelter from the rain anywhere else. These sanitation workers, Memphis' "despised and rejected," had sought sanctuary in Bishop Charles Mason church that night, from the rain, and from the denial of their humanity which was their daily ordeal. What should King choose to say to them?

King said nothing to them; he sang to them. And the first thing he did, was to transport them above the garbage of the streets of Memphis, to the very roof of the universe itself. "Something is happening in Memphis; something is happening in our world. And you know, if I were standing at the beginning of time, with the possibility of taking a kind of general and panoramic view of the whole of human history up to now, and the Almighty said to me, 'Martin Luther King, which age would you like to live in?' I would take my mental flight by Egypt, and I would watch God's children in their magnificent trek from the dark dungeons of Egypt through, or rather across the Red Sea, through the wilderness on toward the Promised Land. And in spite of its magnificence, I wouldn't stop there. I would move on by Greece and take my mind to Mount Olympus. And I would see Plato, Aristotle, Socrates, Euripides and Aristophanes assembled around the Parthenon. And I would watch them around the Parthenon as they discussed the great and eternal issues of reality. But I wouldn't stop there….

"Strangely enough, I would turn to the Almighty and say, 'if you allow me to live just a few years in the second half of the 20th century, I will be happy.' Now that's a strange statement to make, because the world is all messed up. The nation is sick. Trouble is in the land; confusion all around. That's a strange statement. But I know, somehow, that only when it is dark enough can you see the stars."

Poet Percy Shelley, in his essay *A Defense of Poetry*, contends that prophets are poets. "Poets, according to the circumstances of the age and nation in which they appeared, were called, in the earlier epochs of the world, legislators, or prophets: a poet essentially comprises and unites both these characters. For he not only beholds intensely the present as it is, and discovers those laws according to which present things ought to be ordered, but he beholds the future in the present…." Martin Luther King, in that prophetic tradition, brought the sanitation workers that night to the stage of world history, to discuss their cause on that stage, because he recognized that they deserved to be there. When he concluded with the now-world famous "I've Been To The Mountaintop" ending, the reason for its electrifying effect, was that everyone there, for that moment, could see the Promised Land. It was the future in the present, summarized in the final words of King's song: "Mine eyes have seen the glory of the coming of the Lord!!"

That night, and in the last 24 hours of his life, Martin Luther King was the freest man in the United States, perhaps on earth. In our recall of that moment, and that speech, tonight, and in our recall of all the poets and prophets that have done as Martin King, let us remember: "Greater love hath no man than this, that a man lay down his life for his friends."

The Historical Martin Luther King

Ed Asner's opening lines were spoken just after the audience had been involuntarily placed in the position of being the uneasy witnesses to a slave-auction, chanted by baritone Frank Mathis. Mezzo Elvira Green had then performed, solo and without accompaniment, the African-American Spiritual associated with Isabella Baumfree, the Dutch-speaking former slave from upstate New York known as Sojourner Truth, whose refrain, "I told Jesus/ It would be all right/ If he changed my name," was given its context by Asner's commentary.

Abraham Lincoln's 1861-65 War Against the Rebellion; Frederick Douglass and Harriet Tubman's iconic roles in that war; Lincoln's assassination and the onset of segregation after the suppression of the Grant Ad-

ministration's successful efforts to eliminate the Ku Klux Klan; and the resurgence of these efforts in the aftermath of the Second World War, were dramatized in the choral selections, "Battle Cry of Freedom, "Oh! Freedom," and several Spirituals, performed by the chorus and soloists Everett Suttle, Indira Mahajan, Scott Mooney, and the great Simon Estes, one of the most accomplished singers in the history of opera in the world. Asner's narrative's role was to give those unfamiliar with the hundred-year span of history preceding King's 1963-68 "rise and fall," the background to recognize that it was America, not King, that over that time had changed for the worse.

The Classical 'Complex Domain': A Composer's Dialogue on Tragedy

The entirety of the program, however, was actually "anchored, hinged and buttressed" in another musical compositional space entirely, the "sonic footprints" of which were made audible in five musical elements. Those elements were the *Prelude and Fugue in C Minor* by J.S. Bach, BWV 546, played by organist William Trafka; G.W.F. Handel's "And He Shall Feed His Flock," with soprano Indira Mahajan and alto Linda Childs, from Handel's *Messiah;* Beethoven's "Agnus Dei," from his *Mass In C Minor*, Opus 86, with soloists Michelle Fuchs, Nancy Guice, Dante Harrell, and Roger Ham (soprano, alto, tenor, and bass-baritone); the "Lacrymosa" from the Mozart *Requiem,* featuring Indira Mahajan, Linda Childs, Everett Suttle, and Jay Baylon (soprano, alto, tenor, bass-baritone); and "The Trumpet Shall Sound," also from Handel's *Messiah.*

These pieces were actually the expressions of a higher, unseen musical domain, only made "tangible" in the evening's concluding musical and choral selections. An excerpt from the April 3 Mountaintop speech was played to "introduce" the music. The words of Martin Luther King, at his "appointment in Gethsemane," and as spoken by him, rang throughout St. Bartholomew's Church as though he were actually present—because he was. King's voice, always implicit in all that was sung and instrumentally performed by the participating musicians, could be now newly and clearly heard by those that had never known "that side of Martin," and his passionate defense of the poor in his fight for economic justice.

Performances by tenor Everett Suttle of *Round About The Mountain*, and by soprano Osceola Davis of *Guide My Feet*, just prior to King's audio appearance,

April 9 concert in New York commemorating Dr. King.

grounded and buttressed by a selection of familiar Classical compositions that were there to "bear witness" to the aesthetic truth of the life of Rev. Dr. Martin Luther King. Many people, of widely differing backgrounds, have expressed their surprise, excitement and satisfaction with what was presented.

Most importantly, however, twenty-five people signed up to join the New York City Schiller Institute Chorus. The three branches of the chorus, in Manhattan, Brooklyn and Queens, will soon each grow large and strong enough to sustain the growth required to reach the goal of 500 regular members of the chorus. (About 400-500 persons have at one time or another attended a chorus rehearsal.)

It was the chorus that was the spine, the backbone of the entire evening. Diane Sare (*Battle Cry of Freedom* and *Oh! Freedom*) John Sigerson (*Agnus Dei*) and Dr. Roland Carter (all other choral selections) collaborated to weave a singular unity of effect in that respect. Dr. Carter also filled in as pianist for Gregory Hopkins, who had himself acted as an accompanist for other singers on the program.

Dr. Carter, called by one musician "the Ulysses Grant of choral conductors" for his ability to "win vocal victory" against seemingly unfavorable odds, used his arrangement of James Weldon Johnson's *Lift Every Voice And Sing* wisely and well. His arrangement consciously evokes Brahms and other Classical composers, not by plagiarism, or "quoting," but by brandishing the same intent, and therefore the same language. Carter not only involved the entire audience in the performance of the song's first verse, but, having done that, he then insisted that his unique setting of the piece be thoroughly heard by that same audience, which had remained on its feet to hear its conclusion, primarily out of excitement about the intellectual and emotional breakthrough they had just witnessed: No one took out a cell phone for the entire two-hour duration.

underscored and supported the message that was yet to be heard by the audience. Simon Estes' performance of Thomas Dorsey's *Precious Lord*, the song that King requested be played for him literally a few seconds before he was killed, and tenor Gregory Hopkins' surprise rendering of *If I Can Help Somebody*, the lyrics of which King had recited in his famous oration for his own funeral, played on April 9 at Ebenezer Church in Atlanta, were placed just after King's own voice.

As a result of their level of musicianship, and the placement of the successive bass-baritone and then tenor voices, and the subject-matter of the two compositions, the audience heard both of those pieces as though they were direct extensions of not only King's words, but his voice. We had left the domain of musical performance, and had arrived at the domain of music at the service of truth alone.

The Underground Railroad's Conductors

The historical Martin Luther King, rather than the presumptive, non-existent media creation so popularized today, was thus presented to the audience, not in King's own words, but in his intention. The musical arc of the two-hour presentation, while apparently shaped "in the foreground" by the Spirituals, and particularly those conducted by Dr. Roland Carter, was in fact

November 17, 1994

Organizing the Economic Recovery of Eurasia

by Lyndon H. LaRouche, Jr.

The following speech by Mr. LaRouche was written on Nov. 17, 1994, and read for him at a conference in Kiev, Ukraine which took place on Dec. 1-4.

Let me begin by reciting a fact known to us all: *A symptom is not the cause of the disease it expresses.* The present problems of the economy of Ukraine are chiefly a symptom of the fact that the entire world is presently in the grip of a worldwide economic depression. To be precise, a tired and decadent, International Monetary Fund-dominated, global financial system has entered into its collapse-phase. Under these circumstances, the only satisfactory economic policy is a combined set of policy-guidelines and key projects designed to bring about a recovery from the imminent disintegration of the IMF system.

Just as the effects of any epidemic vary somewhat from victim to victim, the recent history of Ukraine affects the way in which the disease expresses itself here, but the underlying sickness is a worldwide epidemic with international causes.

My remarks here are limited to summarizing three points which define the global crisis within which Ukraine is presently trapped. First, a very brief summary, outlining the ongoing, worldwide breakdown of the IMF system. Second, a very brief summary of policies needed to produce economic recoveries in the national economies which are the victims of this collapse. Third, an outline of the proposed key set of infrastructure-building projects needed to bring Eurasia out of the worst crisis of this century.

The Breakdown of the IMF System

Thirty years ago, in the aftermath of the post-missile-crisis nuclear condominium agreements reached among London, Washington, and [Soviet General Secretary Nikita] Khrushchov's Moscow, the powerful, dominant faction of Anglo-American financial capital, led by British Prince Philip's World Wildlife Fund, decided to bring to a close the era of reliance upon investment in scientific and technological progress.

Consequently, during the interval 1964-65, there was a transition to what was often called a "post-industrial" utopia. Over the interval from November 1967 through the London-directed 1973-74 oil-price hoax, and the 1975 Rambouillet monetary conference, the world's monetary and financial system was decoupled from its traditional inter-dependency with the levels of physical output and productivity of labor. Then, beginning with U.S. Federal Reserve Chairman Paul A. Volcker's 1979 introduction of policies which he called the "controlled disintegration of the economy," the world's economically decoupled monetary and financial systems were transformed into a hyperbolic bubble of purely parasitical financial speculation, typified in the extreme, today, in the operations of George Soros's Quantum Fund.

Through the dominant role of the IMF and related institutions, the bulk of the trade and finance of the entire world has been drawn into this bubble of speculation. This global system has now entered the end-phase of its collapse. The collapse itself is already in progress. When the collapse will be completed is still uncertain:

Kiev Conference Seeks Alternative to Shock Therapy

On Dec. 1-4, 1994, a conference, entitled "Social and Economic Problems of Ukraine as a Transitional Society," was held on behalf of and under the auspices of the Supreme Rada (parliament) of Ukraine. Assistance in organizing the conference was provided by the Ukrainian Association of Socio-Economic Development, Management, and Prognosis; the International Center for Policy Studies; the National Academy of Management; the Olzhych Research Foundation; and the Council of Advisers to the parliament of Ukraine.

In addition to a representative of American economist Lyndon LaRouche, representatives of the European Commission, the International Labor Organization in Geneva, the United Nations, the Eastern Europe Institute in Munich, and the World Bank were invited to the conference. Also in attendance were economists from France, Britain, Denmark, Poland, Germany, Italy, and Russia.

The conference took place a few weeks after President Leonid Kuchma and the Ukrainian government began implementing a new round of International Monetary Fund (IMF)-dictated economic shock therapy measures—similar to those that have already failed in Russia. The parliament, under President Olexander Moroz, organized the conference in hopes that it would provide a counterpoint to the shock therapy policies.

Even without the imposition of the latest measures, Ukraine already is suffering a deep economic depression. Hyperinflation, deindustrialization, increasing poverty (especially in the countryside), a rising death rate, and epidemics such as cholera and diphtheria characterize the crisis. Deregulation, privatization, and price liberalization (i.e., price increases) will lead the country into further catastrophe, although the government thinks that it is more clever than the Russians, and that it can avoid the results of shock therapy which occurred there.

The conference was addressed by the head of parliament, Economic Minister Roman Shpek, and head of the State Property Fund Yuriy Yekhanurov, who is in charge of privatization. The latter two speakers gave an ideological defense of IMF conditionalities. Most of the western economists were only moderately critical of the IMF, and were unable to offer a solution to the crisis.

However, Prof. Taras Muranivsky, from the State Humanitarian University in Moscow, and a speech by American economist Lyndon LaRouche, delivered to the conference by a representative of the Schiller Institute, put forward workable alternatives to the IMF policies. Muranivsky spoke about the Russian experience with shock therapy, and the methods of physical economy that are needed in order to get a solution to the crisis, through a program for reconstruction of infrastructure, industry, and the high-technology sector.

It could be a matter of weeks, more probably of months. I am certain that, whether through the alternative of a rational bankruptcy proceeding, or the irrational disintegration of the financial system, the end is now rapidly approaching.

There are only two economic possibilities for each and every part of the world today. The best possibility, is that leading governments use their sovereign political power to put the global system of both monetary and financial institutions into financial bankruptcy. If the governments lack the intelligence or courage to put the existing global system into bankruptcy, the inevitable and early result will be the disintegration of the system brought about through the kind of chain-reaction which can be described fairly by the famous equations for chemical explosions.

In the latter alternative, the result will be chaos, the descent of the entire planet into a dark age worse than that which Europe suffered following the chain-reaction collapse of the Lombard debt-bubble during the middle of the 14th century.

However, if the United States and a few other leading nations react in a sane and courageous way, and put the bankers and speculators into forced bankruptcy reorganization, a general, worldwide economic recovery can be organized immediately. Under those more rational political conditions, an accelerating general economic recovery of Ukraine, and other nations, could be

EIRNS

Independence Square in Kiev. "The present problems of the economy of Ukraine are chiefly a symptom of the fact that the entire world is presently in the grip of a worldwide economic depression."

launched. If we take the view that such an alternative to chaos will be forthcoming, then we can take certain immediate steps now which prepare the way for that kind of general economic recovery.

I focus now upon that policy perspective.

Recovery as a Renaissance

A few historical facts about the modern western european economy point to the kind of recovery measures which will be successful under present world conditions.

It is useful to describe the global economic collapse now in progress as the end of a centuries-long dynasty of modern european civilization, what had been the most powerful civilization which ever existed up until the present moment. It must be our purpose to discover what was right, and what was wrong in that western european dynasty which came to dominate this planet. What was the source of that civilization's great power; what were the causes of its presently ongoing collapse. From this vantage-point, an economic recovery is to be seen as an economic renaissance, a revival of the good principles of european civilization, but minus the foolish principles which have brought about the collapse.

For example, prior to A.D. 1440, the population of this planet never exceeded several hundred million persons. The level of productive technology reached prior to the 15th-century Renaissance did not permit the human species to reach the potential population density needed to rise above a few hundred million. More than 90% of the human population of all cultures lived in a condition which may be fairly described as brutish misery, that of serfs or slaves. The source of the power which enabled the culture of western Europe to achieve world domination were three revolutionary changes in political institutions which were introduced approximately the middle of the 15th century: the idea of the modern nation-state republic, the principle of generalized scientific progress, and the general commitment to investing in the fruits of scientific and technological progress for the increase of the productive powers of mankind per capita, per household, and per square kilometer of land-area.

The trouble has been, the stubborn persistence of those feudal traditions of oligarchism and usury which, unfortunately, came to dominate the political and financial institutions and policies of the most powerful states within the orbit of western european culture. It is the triumph of usurious financial speculation over technological progress in both basic economic infrastructure and physical production, which is the specific cause for the presently ongoing doom of the existing global monetary and financial systems.

We see that, since 1989, the levels of output in the former Comecon sector have fallen to less than 30% of their levels under the former communist regimes. The specific cause for this collapse has been the policies of reform which were imposed upon the former Comecon sector, first by Britain's Prime Minister Margaret Thatcher, U.S. President George Bush, and the International Monetary Fund. These states received from Thatcher, Bush, and the IMF all of the bad features of a dying western european civilization, and virtually none of the advantages.

One might say that the peoples of eastern Europe spent decades traversing the vast desert of socialism, to arrive finally at the gates of a powerful city. They arrived tired, famished, and thirsty, hoping to find a better, freer life. Instead, they arrived at the time that city, ruled by madmen, was struck by a savage epidemic against which the arriving people had no developed resistance.

In the science of physical economy founded by Gottfried Leibniz, the measure of prosperity is the number of persons who can be sustained with improved health, increased life-expectancy, with greater potential population-density. This accomplishment is made possible by two interdependent means. First, the general application of advances in science and technology to increase the productive powers of labor per capita and per square kilometer. Second, those improvements in land which must be made and sustained to absorb these advances in productive technology.

Voluntaristic Creativity and the State

The accomplishment of modern western european civilization was to discover that the realization of improvements in technology was better obtained through utilizing the factor of voluntaristic creativity, under the institution of private entrepreneurship in agriculture and industry, but, that the potential success of such private entrepreneurship required the state's responsibility for providing and maintaining those necessary improvements in land-area we know as basic economic infrastructure. This was the form of capitalist development we find in the United States of Presidents George Washington and Abraham Lincoln, and the Germany of the Humboldt brothers and Friedrich List.

The most successful growth of industrial capitalism occurred when this division of labor between the state sector of the economy and the entrepreneurial sector was applied. The most efficient mechanisms were as follows. First, the state exerted its responsibility for a monopoly in the creation, issuance, and protection of the national currency. This issuance of currency served as the backbone of the public credit supplied to both the state and private sectors through a national banking system. This primary issuance of new credit was made available to selected classes of responsible borrowers at low borrowing costs. These loans were concentrated in enterprises of the public sector, including credit supplied to contractors participating in those public works of infrastructure-building. That provided the stimulant of growth for the private sector as a whole.

Military expenditures to one side, the role of the public sector of the econmy is made intelligible by considering the following highlights. The essential categories of basic economic infrastructure are of two types. The first type has the form of the improvement of land: water management, general transportation, power, sanitation, and public communications. The second type is represented by those social services indispensable for developing and maintaining the productive powers of labor: education, health care, and science. Both types are primarily the responsibility of the state sector. The level of development of both categories of infrastructure, per household and per square kilometer, is a measure of the potential for realizing the lifting of the productive powers of labor to some specific level.

For example, given any level of productive technology, we can measure the requirements of power and water for agriculture and for industries. Water and rail transport are the cheapest and most efficient modes of medium-range transport of goods, by a large margin of advantage over any other modes of transport. By comparing the maps of power, water, water-transport, rail-transport for various nations today, we are showing the relative economic potential for industries and farms located in the various regions and localities of the maps. There is a similar case for the locations of schools, medical facilities, and centers of scientific research and practice. Thus, in the history of successful cases of economic growth, the development of infrastructure preceded and stimulated the successful development of farms and industries.

Economic Development Programs

For that reason, over the years, my associates and I have designed a number of large-scale economic-development programs, including that which we proposed in late 1989 and 1990 for the United States, and western european assistance for the rapid development of the economies of the eastern european nations.

Our design for eastern Europe was centered in the part of Europe which has the highest density of infrastructure development, and the highest productivity (**Figure 1**). This is an approximate spherical triangle which runs from Paris down to Vienna, up to Berlin, and back to Paris by way of the German Ruhr region and Lille. From this "Productive Triangle," as we have named it, we specified corridors of rail-centered infrastructural development reaching out to the south and east (**Figure 2**).

Back in 1984, we had already designed and published policy proposals for the development of the land areas bordering the Pacific and Indian oceans. Now, beginning in 1989, our concern was to link the development of the european "Productive Triangle" beyond the

The European 'Productive Triangle' Area

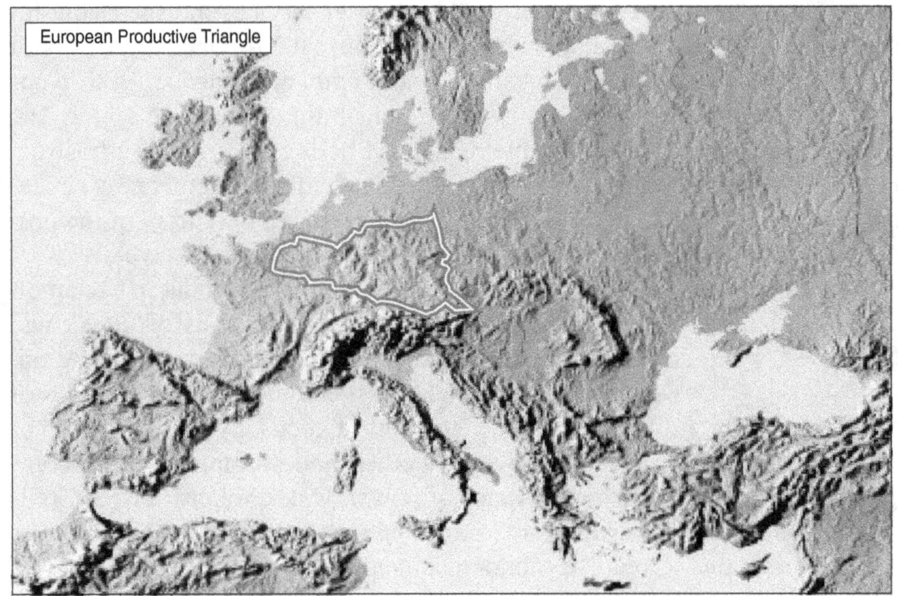

This area of Europe has the highest concentration of productive power in the world. Ensuring proper investment and infrastructure development here is key to boosting productivity and ensuring peak functioning, vital for leading an economic recovery worldwide.

FIGURE 2
Proposed European 'Productive Triangle' Rail Development

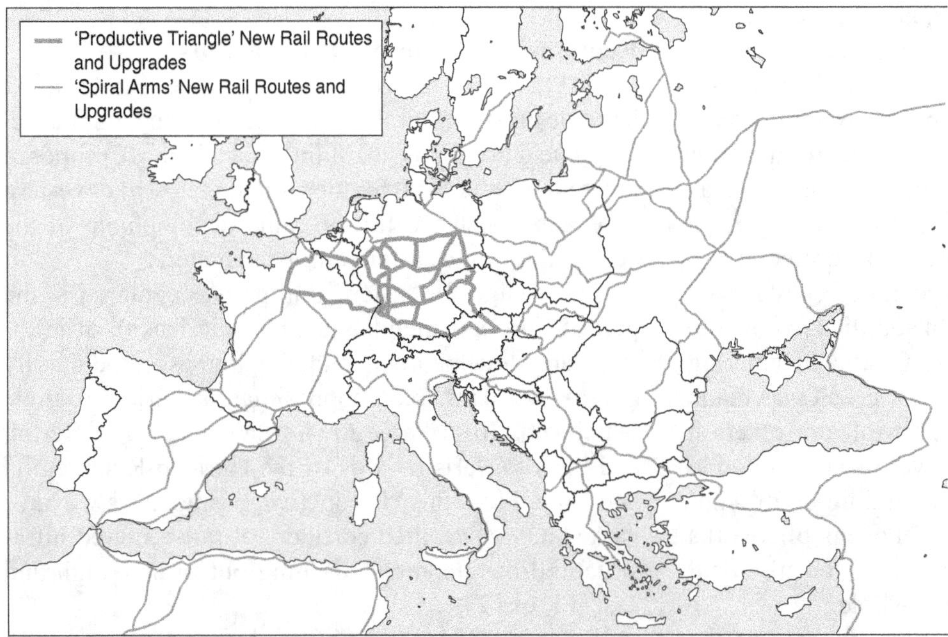

The European "Productive Triangle" of high-speed rail lines and intensive infrastructure investment was proposed by LaRouche after the Berlin Wall fell in 1989. It encompasses an area whose vertices are Paris, Berlin, and Vienna. "Spiral arms," or corridors of development, would extend to Scandinavia; eastern Europe, Russia, Ukraine, and farther east to Asia; the Balkans and the Middle East; and to Iberia and North Africa.

Balkans and Russia, through rail links into East and South Asia. It is now clear that others were thinking similarly (**Figure 3**). Since April 1975, we have been committed to the securing of Arab-Palestinian peace through cooperative economic development of the Middle East (**Figure 4**). During the 1970s and 1980s, we also worked with relevant institutions in the development of similar proposals for parts of Africa (**Figure 5**) and the Americas. Here, **Figure 6**, from a South America project. Here, **Figure 7**, one sees reflected our modification of an engineering design for general water and power development plan for North America.

Government-Created Credit

In the best possible situation which might exist anywhere in the world a short time ahead, most of the world's central banking systems and financial institutions will be either closed down, or operating under rules of government-supervised financial reorganization. Under such conditions, to speak of an economic recovery which relies upon private lenders for investments, is a very cruel joke to play upon the people of any nation. Only sovereign governments can create the masses of new credit needed to halt a catastrophe.

If that government-created new credit is provided and used in the right way, it will be a noninflationary stimulant for rapid progress through full employment and growth of the private sector in agriculture, industry, and commerce. The foundation of this recovery must be higher priorities

Proposed 'Eurasian Land Bridge' Rail Development

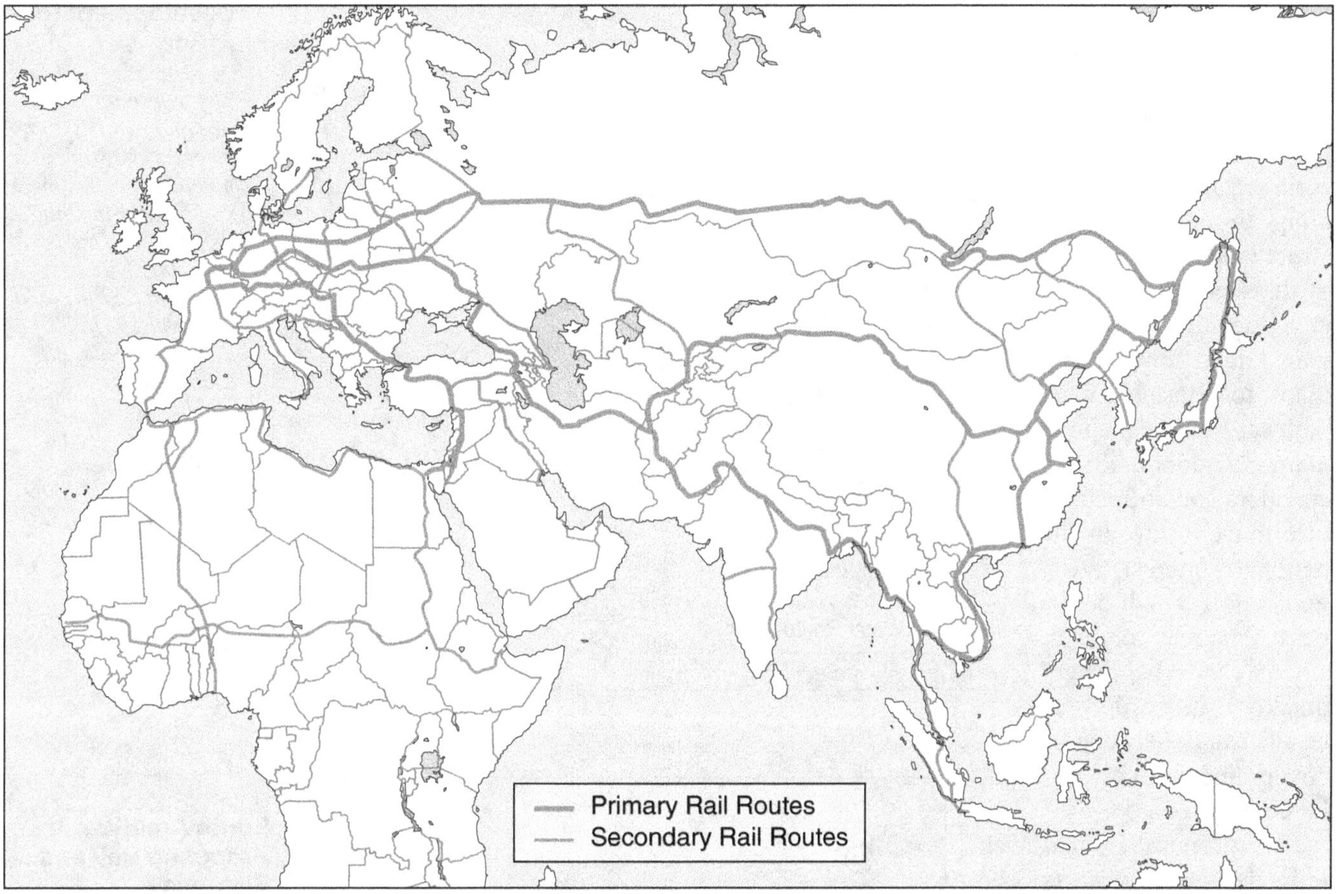

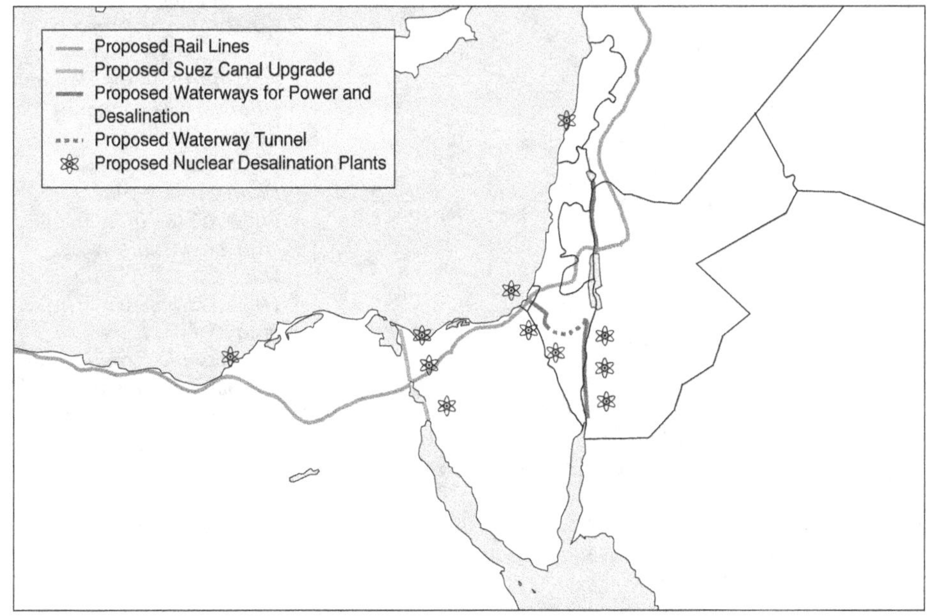

LaRouche's 'Oasis Plan' for Development of the Middle East Crossroads

High-speed and maglev rail corridors form the Eurasian land bridge. Rail lines from France to Africa, and to Russia and China, and into Japan, were the 1896 "Great Project" of France's Gabriel Hanotaux and Russia's Sergei Witte. The northern route is the Trans-Siberian line; farther south, the new Silk Road line branches into China and India; the third main trunk goes to the Mideast and Africa.

Lyndon LaRouche's "Oasis Plan" for the Mideast features canals linking the Mediterranean with the Dead Sea and/or the Red Sea to Dead Sea to provide freshwater for agriculture, industry, and domestic use. Shown are the general locations for nuclear-powered desalination facilities to provide freshwater; in effect, a new Jordan River.

for large-scale programs of building up basic economic infrastructure, and issuing necessary credit for payrolls and materials to private entrepreneurs who win contracts to assist in creating those new infrastructure developments.

It is not difficult for any logistic specialists who know how to read maps, to determine what pathways on the map the main corridors and sub-corridors of infrastructure must follow in the national interest. Any good choices will be the best practical choices, since we must begin very quickly, in order to ensure a national economic recovery and recovery of popular confidence.

My proposal is, that such infrastructure projects be planned now, and some parts of the projects actually begun. As most of us are painfully aware, at present, with the continued dominant role of the City of London and International Monetary Fund in determining what is allowed or not allowed in the economies of any part of eastern Europe today, large-scale infrastructural programs will be either sabotaged, or openly forbidden by these monetary and financial authorities. Once the financial system crashes, which will be soon, those authorities will be either nonexistent or very much weakened politically. It is important to plant the seeds of the future

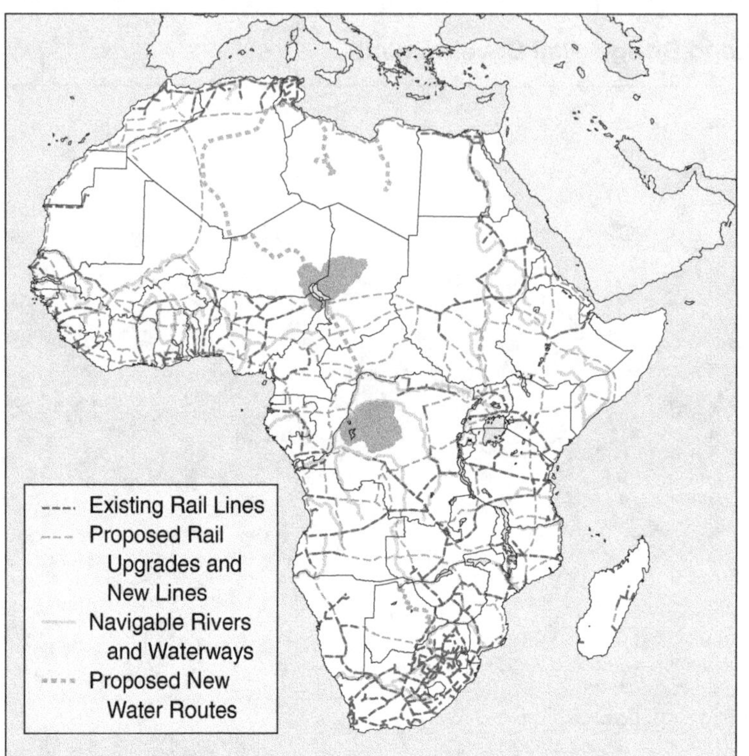

FIGURE 5

Rail and Waterway Development for Africa

The transcontinental rail and priority water projects show the vast potential for this huge continent. Finishing the Jonglei Canal on the White Nile in southern Sudan could add over 5% to the flow of the Nile. All such projects, combined with nuclear-powered development complexes, would be the basis for billions more people.

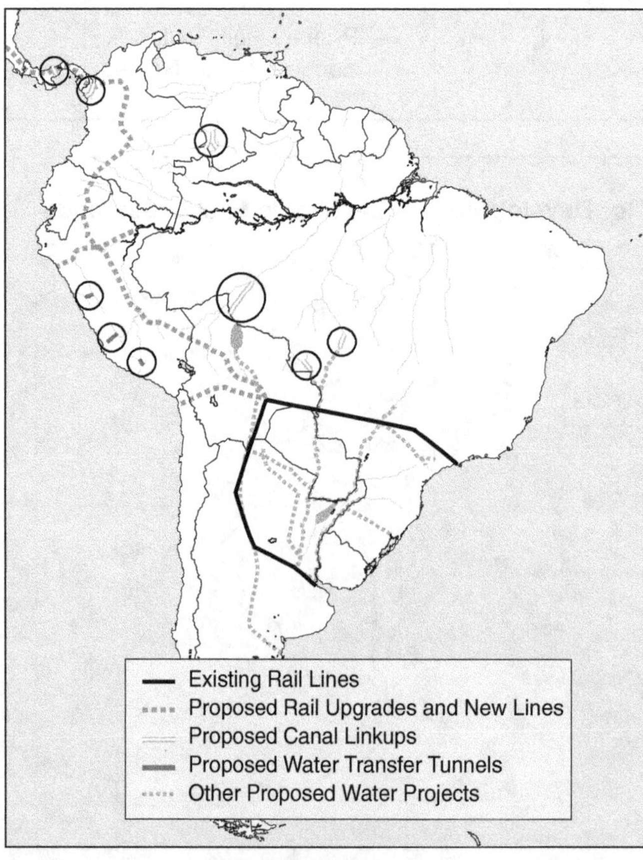

FIGURE 6

South America: Proposed Rail and Waterway Development

Existing and proposed water and rail projects include a new interoceanic canal through the Panama Isthmus. The Orinoco-Amazon River canal and the Amazon-Rio de la Plata canal would integrate the three huge river basins, allowing ships to operate over 10,000 kilometers. The dream of the Pan-American Railroad would be completed as a high-speed rail system.

large-scale projects now, by proceeding with useful smaller portions of those projects.

As I have described this proposed policy elsewhere, think of this as a process of building a bridge from Hell to Purgatory. Build the first foundations of that bridge on this side of the chasm today, and so assemble the cadres needed to put through the completion of the project on an expanded basis, once the political opposition to economic recovery has been neutralized by its own bankruptcy.

North America: Water Development (NAWAPA)

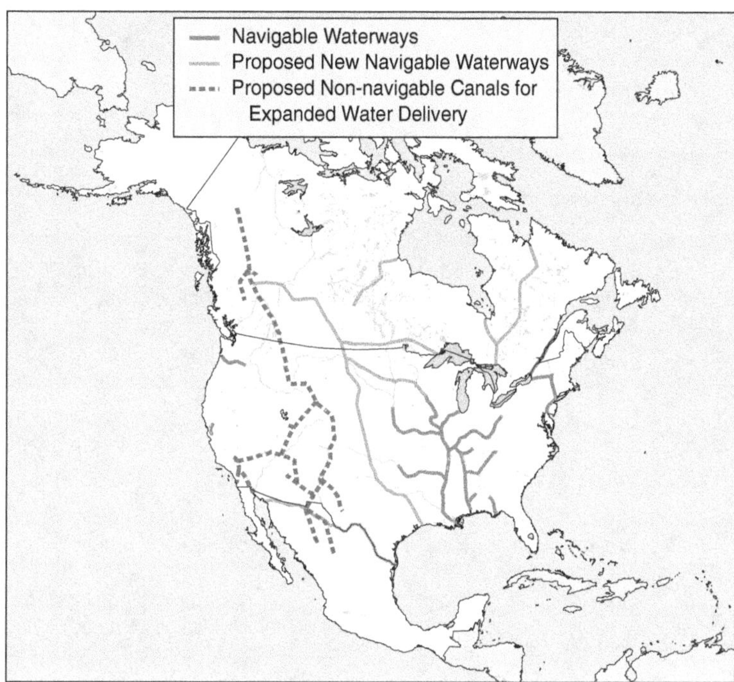

The North American Water and Power Alliance (Nawapa). This 1960s engineering plan by the Ralph M. Parsons Co. would divert enough unused water now flowing north to the Arctic, southward through a natural and engineered Rocky Mountain Trench, to bring a new supply of 135 billion gallons a day to the Canadian and U.S. plains, the Great Lakes, and Mexico.

FIDELIO

Journal of Poetry, Science, and Statecraft

From the first issue, dated Winter 1992, featuring Lyndon LaRouche on "The Science of Music: The Solution to Plato's Paradox of 'The One and the Many,'" to the final issue of Spring/Summer 2006, a "Symposium on Edgar Allan Poe and the Spirit of the American Revolution," *Fidelio* magazine gave voice to the Schiller Institute's intention to create a new Golden Renaissance.

The title of the magazine, is taken from Beethoven's great opera, which celebrates the struggle for political freedom over tyranny. *Fidelio* was founded at the time that LaRouche and several of his close associates were unjustly imprisoned, as was the opera's Florestan, whose character was based on the American Revolutionary hero, the French General, Marquis de Lafayette.

Each issue of *Fidelio*, throughout its 14-year lifespan, remained faithful to its initial commitment, and offered original writings by LaRouche and his associates, on matters of, what the poet Percy Byssche Shelley identified as, "profound and impassioned conceptions respecting man and nature."

Back issues are now available for purchase through the Schiller Institute website:
http://schillerinstitute.org/about/order_form.html